The Bernese Mountain Dog

A DOG OF DESTINY

BERND GUENTER

Dr. Bernd Guenter is an internationally published German dog writer and photographer whose work emphasizes a responsible and happy companionship between humans and dogs. For over two decades, he has lived a full life with the Bernese Mountain Dog and has been actively committed to the welfare of this magnificent breed. His book, *Berner Sennenhund,* now in its fifth edition, has received unanimous and enthusiastic praise from the canine press and from Bernese breed clubs. Guenter also enjoys recognition as the premier photographer of the Bernese Mountain Dog. His images uniquely capture the breathtaking beauty—body and soul—of the Berner Sennenhund as well as the wonder of the human-Berner bond.

Bernd Guenter is a long-standing member of the Bernese Mountain Dog Clubs of America, Canada, Great Britain, Switzerland, and, of course, Germany. As a guardian of the breed, he has supported numerous Bernese educational and welfare projects. He is honored to be a member of the *Dog Writers Association of America* and the *World Dog Press Association.* Bernd and his wife, Christa, share their life and their Black Forest home with their current Berner partner, Mika.

Book editor: MaryEllen Smith
Cover & interior design: 1106 Design

ISBN: 0-9745407-3-0
Library of Congress Control Number: 2004101441

This is the author's translation of his book *Berner Sennenhund*
© Kynos Verlag Dr. Dieter Fleig GmbH, 1993; 5th ed. 2004
Mürlenbach/Germany
www.kynos-verlag.de

Contents

Many books are written about dogs. Some come from the point of view of the pet owner, others are devoted to showing dogs, and yet others to dog health and maintenance, kennel management, locomotion and function, or training. Still others are tales about the lives of dogs and their people.

This book covers all those topics, but is still more. It is a splendidly illustrated book about life with a dog; in fact, it is about living life to its fullest with a dog. The dog in question happens to be a Bernese Mountain Dog, and there is a good deal of information in this book that is particular to this breed. However, this is more than a breed book. It is about enriching the life of the dog and its people in diverse ways, including understanding the historical and functional perspectives of the breed. It is about making the correct decisions on selecting a breed with which to share one's life, about raising the dog and training it and its people, about deciding whether to compete in the show ring with the dog, and about whether or not to breed it. But mostly it is a warm, thoughtful, sensitive study about the daily life, needs, and activities of a dog and its people.

This is a responsible book—no, a Bernese Mountain Dog is not the dog for all people; it is a truthful book—yes, Bernese puppies can be destructive and aggravating; but above all, it is a beautiful book—for the right people, there can be no better friendship than that between mutually devoted people and their dog. Although this devotion is lifelong, it is, of course, too short in the case of the dog.

The author of this engaging book, Bernd Guenter, is also a superb photographer whose devotion to Berners shines through his visual documentation as well as his prose.

—Dr. Mary Dawson
Charter Member and First Elected President
Bernese Mountain Dog Club of America

CHAPTER 1

Meet The Bernese Mountain Dog

FIRST IMPRESSION: A CANINE BEAUTY EXTRAORDINAIRE

A dog (let's call him Max.) A dog of spectacular beauty and imposing stature: large, powerful, compact, and sturdily built, yet harmoniously proportioned. Everything about him seems to be perfectly balanced, from his strong limbs on round feet to his mighty chest and broad, firm back. His softly rounded rump accommodates a long, bushy tail that hangs when in repose, but becomes an extension of the back when trotting.

Max is a good 50 kg (110 lbs.) of muscular, controlled strength that he carries with athletic grace. His height at the shoulders is 66 cm (26 in.)—a body only slightly longer than it is tall. A powerful, wide, yet by no means coarse head is borne proudly on a strong neck of moderate length. His triangular ears are short, flat, lie close to his head, and are lightly feathered; powerful teeth complement his majestic head. Max's long, gently waved, shiny coat is comprised of a fascinating symmetry of colors—black, white, and rust. Jet black is the ground color, while a white blaze adds kindness, charm, and friendliness to the face. Russet spots above his dark-brown eyes and on the cheeks form cheerful, lively accent marks. When his mouth opens a little, one gets the impression of a smile. On the legs, rust markings connect the black and white. The white chest, visible at a distance even in the dark, adds a touch of brightness that is pleasant and reassuring. White feet provide elegance when standing and grace in motion. The white tail tip is the perfect accent to this perfect harmony of colors. The beauty of the dog's physical structure is further enhanced by his regal bearing; the gently measured and smooth, powerful movement; and the dignified and kindly expression. In short, this is a beauty of a dog, and beauty has a name: the Bernese Mountain Dog.

The Bernese is a dog for
all reasons and all seasons

Scenes of everyday life:
a dream of a dog—at home

It is six o'clock in the morning. Max is dreaming on his comfy blanket beside the bed where his folks sleep. A sound from outside breaks the early morning stillness. Footsteps approach the house, come to a halt, something metal claps shut, and the footsteps recede: it was the newspaper man. Max has noticed, of course, but there is no reason for him to open his eyes, let alone react to it in any other way.

Later that day, the sun is shining. Max lies lazily in the grass, close to the house. Without his folks he never moves a step further away; leaving the premises on his own would never occur to him, although there may be times when the gate is left open. And he would never jump the fence, although it is only 1.2 m (4 ft.) high—just two simple boards on poles (see photo p. 15), and thus no real obstacle for an agile Berner. He gives passing pedestrians an attentive eye and maybe a raised eyebrow, but they are hardly ever worth a bark. Max watches youngsters playing soccer on the other side of the fence with a calm and benevolent interest. Suddenly the ball bounces into the yard. Max raises his head. One of the children, a boy of perhaps nine years, steps up to the fence and says, "Hi, Max!" as he climbs over, picks up the ball, and returns to his game. He knows his way. Max has moved only an eyebrow. The little boy had his permission, dictated by instinct and reinforced by education, to climb over the fence to retrieve the ball; the boy's eighteen-year-old brother would have been given a different, less friendly, and more vocal welcome.

After lunch, Max is napping inside. A strange car stops in front of the house, and a man gets out and approaches the gate. Max jumps up and gives two dark, impressive warning barks. As the man opens the gate, enters the yard, and ascends the steps, Max—who has been watching him through the little window alongside the door—barks angrily and hurls the weight of his powerful body against the unbreakable glass. This is the only time his voice is heard that day. As soon as the stranger is admitted and welcomed as a guest, Max quiets and calms down. Throughout the entire visit he lies, discreet yet fully attentive, between the stranger and his folks.

When the humans arrive home after a long, hard day at work, they are tired, worn-out, and irritable. An argument begins for no real reason; voices rise and get sharper. Max steps like an umpire between his parents, and with wagging tail and nudging nose demands and restores peace. Max dislikes arguments and quarrels in his house and abhors sharp voices. Peace and quiet return. Soon four hands are petting him accompanied by a spoken "Thank you, Max!"

Later that night, Max reclines at his humans' feet—where else?—as they watch television. Suddenly there is a noise out in the hallway, the door opens, and a stranger is standing there with a raised arm and something grasped in his hand. With lightning speed and a thunderous growl, Max jumps at the intruder, grabs his arm and keeps a grip on it, even when the unknown human's other arm brings the rubber truncheon down on his back. Only at a command from his master does he release his powerful jaws. Max has just passed, with flying colors, a test that had been arranged with a trainer from a local dog obedience club. Max's protective instinct proved effective and sound, even though he has never received any *Schutzhund* (protection dog) training (which includes tracking, obedience, and protection).

The next day is Sunday—a perfect morning for a leisurely breakfast. As always at mealtime, Max is lying near his folks with his head turned away from the table. The smell of Black Forest ham and other tasty breakfast meats, soft-boiled eggs, fresh crusty rolls and local honey is of no (apparent) interest to him; he knows that nothing ever falls off the table. Then all of a sudden he sits up and, gently but insistently, pushes his big, soft, warm muzzle under his mistress's arm, almost causing coffee to spill from the cup in her hand. That is his way of signaling that he wishes to be patted and stroked. His desire for physical affection, hands-on tenderness, and a gentle caress is immense, and his way of expressing this need is unmistakable. Who could possibly resist when such a giant teddy bear sits on one's feet, leaning his mighty back against one's legs, throwing his head back and offering his soft throat for petting?

Outdoors

Max's human is following Max on their daily morning walk across the fields. The white tip of the dog's tail moves through the dense fog like a guiding light. Then suddenly it disappears. Max has gone off to relieve himself in privacy. There is no reason for his human to worry, or to change his pace or direction; he knows that in a moment's time the dog will return to him. Max can be trusted not to stray.

While walking through the nearby forest, Max, off-leash as usual, alternately ambles leisurely just a little behind his human, or takes the lead by a few steps, exploring the territory. Suddenly, a short distance ahead of them, a deer steps out of the undergrowth and stands still, eyeing them curiously and cautiously. Both human and Max stop in their tracks immediately, as if guided by some common internal force. With the respect and modesty that befits them as guests, they stand watching the inhabitant of the forest. When the deer disappears a few moments later, the two move on. Max never leaves a forest trail, unless he needs to relieve himself.

Strolling between fields and meadows, Max sniffs his way along, dodging puddles, sidestepping the scat his cousins have left on the trail. Then he begins to trot; moving faster, he shifts into high gear, gallops across a field, and paces up and down along the edge of a freshly plowed field until he has found the perfect spot. Relieving himself on trails, sidewalks, or curbsides is something Max detests (and his humans would not allow anyway).

A little later, a group of panting joggers approach ahead. When Max catches their eye, they hesitate (experience may have taught them to be wary). Inquiring human eyes establish contact and a reassuring nod signals "No problem!" Max, preoccupied with tempting wayside smells, does not even lift his head as the joggers continue on their way. As they pass by, one of them pats him on the head.

Just before the trail takes a blind bend, a short whistle comes from his human. Max stops, turns around, and waits until his friend is by his side. As soon as it is plain that the space just ahead is clear, the human voices a low word, and Max is again free to ramble. A woman comes along, accompanied by a little dog. Seeing Max, she scoops her tiny companion up in her arms, obviously afraid for his safety. A few friendly words and a smile from Max's human reestablish the woman's confidence. She puts her sweetheart down again and watches with amazement and delight the mighty Berner's gentle and patient tolerance of his miniature cousin's yappy playfulness.

Life in human society

The door of the restaurant opens and Max, on a short lead, accompanies his humans inside. Even before they are properly seated, Max has settled under the table—this is obviously not a first for him. A friendly waitress brings him a bowl of water. During the meal, Max is a quiet companion; there is no raising of his head, sniffing around, or begging for table scraps. Afterwards all three leave the restaurant as they entered—disciplined, calm, and quiet. Well-behaved canine guests like Max are usually welcome in restaurants and hotels in most parts of Europe. Max knows, of course, that he will get a treat outside; this is his reward for having displayed impeccable table manners.

Saturday morning, downtown. Max, as usual, accompanies his humans; this time, however, he is on a leash. Although he had already relieved himself at home before they came to town, one of his humans carries a poop bag, just in case. A stroll through town with Max is a happy but time-consuming event. Max is—like every Berner—a crowd-stopper, always attracting lots of attention. Many friendly, interested, and admiring eyes rest on him. People stop and stare, often saying "what a beauuutiful dog!" Questions are asked about his name, his breed, his temperament, how much and what he eats, how much he weighs, how often he needs to be brushed. People from all walks of life wish to pet him—and they may. Children of all ages are introduced to him, and their little hands pat him, grab him, and caress him. Peachy baby cheeks touch his velvety ear flaps; toddlers' faces sink into that soft Berner fur. Max bears all the attention with regal calm, charming friendliness, and saintly patience. And when it hurts—when tiny fingers poke his nose or careless little feet step on his toes—he simply moves aside.

At the veterinarian's. Inside the waiting room are some canine cousins, plus a variety of other pets: a hamster, a budgie, a rabbit, and two cats. On a short leash and heeling closely, Max enters with his human and they both take a seat. Max lies there calmly, without any sign of anxiety, watching the others with detached interest until the receptionist says "Next, please!" As usual, he steps first onto the scale. No change in weight—that's good! Next he enters the examining room for a few sniffs and a tail-wagging greeting for his old friend, the vet, and his assistant before the familiar procedure begins: stethoscope, otoscope, ophthalmoscope, dental check, blood sample, rabies shot, etc. Result: everything's okay. At well over 10 years of age, Max is still in immaculate health and top condition.

On New Year's Eve, with friends. After a midnight toast, everyone goes outside to enjoy the fireworks. Needless to say, Max is with them, unimpressed even by the distant cannon's noise and the popping and lights of the fireworks nearby.

While these are actual everyday scenes from Max's life, they also describe the ideal character of a Bernese Mountain Dog: friendly, good-natured, affectionate, gentle, and sensitive, he is happiest in an intimate, closely-bonded family relationship and most content when inside the home. He is self-confident, stable, patient, tolerant, calm, balanced, laid-back, and poised in any situation, with a high threshold for stimulation and a quick return to calm if he does become excited. He is also reliable, attentive, alert, vigilant, fearless, and—if the situation requires—protective.

The bottom line is that this is an absolute dream of a dog. He is of venerable age, in excellent health, and possesses an impeccable temperament and breathtaking beauty. He is a happy dog— with happy humans. Max is lucky, too, because an element of luck was necessary. That adorable, snuggly teddy bear of a puppy could have grown into a nervous, insecure, spooky, jumpy, hand-shy, fear-biting wimp, or a dominant-aggressive monster that threatened other dogs as well as his own human family. He could have been plagued with health problems ranging from incorrect dentition to painful entropion to crippling hip or elbow dysplasia. He could have suffered an early, shockingly fast, painful death of bloat, or an anticipated, extended, slow and excruciating death of cancer. But Max was lucky—and his humans are blessed.

The dream must be assisted

Four crucial factors must converge to make the perfect Bernese:

1. The breed's heritage. This is the cumulative result of centuries of effort of breeders and, more recently, breed clubs, who have worked to develop, foster, and preserve the Berner *Sennenhund*.
2. A specific breeder's responsible, committed endeavor to bring out the very best of the breed through careful, knowledgeable selection of parent dogs in order to create the ideal representative of the breed.
3. Luck, pure and simple.

4. The Berner's humans, whose lives the dog will share, and who will be either a blessing or a curse to him.

If all four factors combine, the ideal result will be a perfect Berner in the finest health with an impeccable temperament, a long life expectancy, and beautiful conformation. The element of luck plays a major role when it comes to health, longevity, and conformation, regardless of the breeder's scrupulousness and conscientiousness in breeding, raising, caring, feeding, and providing the best possible environment. It is with deliberation and reason that this author ranks the aspect of beauty last.

Temperament is the area that is least dependent on luck. Regardless of genetics, a dog is not born a fear biter, dominant pack leader, or ferociously aggressive monster. Nor is every Bernese Mountain Dog born a tolerant friend of children, a reliable companion, a calm and imperturbable cohort, a trustworthy heeler, or a willing drafter. It is a well-established fact that temperament is a combination of inherited traits and acquired behavior. The former is genetically determined and thus can only be influenced to a limited extent by breeding strategies. The latter, however, is subject to the total control, and is hence the full responsibility, of humans.

Inadequate and insufficient education prevents positive character traits from developing or causes them to wither; competent education may compensate for existing weaknesses and bring out the best in a dog. Not even Max was born the ideal Berner that he is. His humans' happiness was by no means always unmitigated. There were the first days in his new home when Max piddled on the Oriental rug in the living room, chewed the leg of his master's easy chair, ripped down a curtain in the dining room, and left deep toenail scratches on the front door. Then came the weeks when, left unsupervised, he shredded his mattress, dug many deep holes in the yard, chewed on flowers and shrubs, and discovered that there was just enough room under the fence for him to squeeze through. And there were times when the little rascal just would not come when called; when he picked up, with obvious delight, empty cigarette packs, used tissues, bits of styrofoam, plastic bags, or virtually anything litterbugs had left behind; when, at any attempt by his humans to take the stuff away from him, he sneeringly zigzagged off, looking back with unmasked glee, hoping to provoke a chase from a safe distance; when he snatched horse muffins and sheep droppings and—at the approach of his humans—quickly swallowed them, licking his lips with relish; when he rolled happily and with visible delight in a freshly manured meadow; when he caused embarrassment and anger by jumping up, with muddy paws, on unsuspecting pedestrians; when in a short span of weeks he chewed through three safety belts in the car while his folks were shopping; and when he protested against being left alone at home with such heart-rending screams that the neighbors suspected a cow was calving. In such hard times, luck will not help.

Training is the name of the game. On the humans' part this requires patience, a willingness to learn, and absolutely consistent behavior paired with unwavering persistence, always treating the dog responsibly, foregoing cherished habits, and much, much time. To be blessed with a healthy, long-lived, beautiful Bernese Mountain Dog, is—beyond all conscientious circumspection of breeders and breed clubs—a gift of good fortune. To have a good and happy Berner, however, is not the result of luck. A dog that is good and happy is the direct result of his humans' responsible and intelligent actions. Through intensive and consistent care for and interaction with the dog from the very first moment, one can and must establish the foundation for a happy lifelong partnership. This foundation can be defined as teaching the dog to find his way around your world—the human world, which is strange to a canine—without conflict and collisions. However, at the same time, you must be careful not to deprive the dog of his identity as a dog, nor of his individual personality. Adaptation: yes. Suppression: no!

Bonding—Berner-style

This requires, of course, that one understand the otherness of the canine being; one must comprehend the characteristics of the canine mind, emotions, and actions. On the basis of this understanding, one must seek out and find the ways and means that will enable the dog to successfully master the necessary processes of learning, familiarization, and adaptation. In other words, man must become the dog's mentor and, as such, must make learning as easy as possible for the dog. Since a dog is not only a member of its species, but also an individual, one must at the same time recognize, foster, and shape the dog's individuality.

To learn about the dog, and to teach him and help him to learn, is a process that simultaneously requires and produces one result: a close partnership between human and dog. The more trusting the relationship between dog and human, the more successful the teaching of the dog will be. By the same token, the more thoroughly you pursue the training of your dog, the closer the relationship between you and the dog will become. The better a dog is educated, the better he will be able to function in the human world, and thus will become a more reliable partner for his humans.

Human and dog exist in a state of mutual dependence. You render yourself voluntarily dependent, to a degree that you determine, on the dog. Your decision to share your life with a dog is a commitment to accept responsibility for the dog's welfare and well-being. The more aware you are of your responsibility and of the consequences your actions will have on the dog, the more seriously

A well-mannered Berner is the perfect shopping buddy

you will take this responsibility and the more dependent you will make yourself. The reward for this dependence is priceless; it is the wonderful experience of living in perfect harmony and total happiness with your canine partner/family member.

The dog's dependence on his human is different in both degree and kind. It is involuntary and total. The dog is what his human makes him. The act of "making" equals power; man has power over the dog. This power must never be abused. On the contrary, one must consciously limit one's own power by basing its use on the careful consideration and awareness of one's responsibility for the dog's well-being, which will, in turn, accrue to one's benefit. The sooner and the better the dog learns to live with his humans, the less problematic, the more satisfying, and the more rewarding their partnership will be. Training is the basis of communication between human and dog. When this communication does not function effectively, insecurity will grow which will lead to mistakes. The resultant mistakes will repeatedly, and increasingly severely, impair communication. Functioning communication between you and your dog is the absolute prerequisite to the dog becoming certain of you, and your becoming certain of your dog. You both need this certainty. Each must be completely predictable to the other. A dog that is not certain of his human will, in critical situations, avoid him or—at best—ignore him. At worst he will rebel against his human and will resist him by his own means. A human who is not certain of his dog will constantly be subjected to negative experiences and emotions, including (but not limited to) stress, anxiety, irritation, anger, helplessness, embarrassment, and feelings of failure and guilt. Conversely, however, the sooner and the better a dog learns to function in human society, the more freedom he can be granted to be himself. The more certain you are of your dog, the more relaxed you can be about allowing your dog the freedom to be his real dog-self in the canine world. You can allow him to move around freely, to enjoy experiences, and to live according to his natural impulses and joys, from sniffing out a meadow undisturbed to meeting fellow canines unhindered.

A well-socialized Berner is a reliable babysitter—even with the smallest of his charges

It goes without saying that this partnership between human and dog allows no room for force, or fear, or aggression. The elements that shape and sustain the human-canine partnership are mutual love, mutual trust, and mutual respect. The latter element is of particular importance. People who do not respect their dog do not deserve him. Someone who is not prepared to honor the personality of his dog should not have him. Although a person who has no respect for his dog may be able to break him in—that is, to make him obedient, to turn the puppy into a puppet—they will never be able to educate him. It must also be unmistakably stated that in describing the relationship between human and dog, terms such as "to keep" or "to own"—although they are legally valid and commonly used—are blatantly out of place. One does not own a dog, but is his caregiver and companion. One does not keep a dog; one lives with him.

People unwilling or unable to adapt their own attitudes and lifestyles accordingly will be better off without a dog—and the dog will most certainly be better off without them. While this is universally true for every dog, it bears special relevance to the Bernese Mountain Dog.

An extraordinary dog for extraordinary people

The Bernese Mountain Dog is different from most other dogs in many respects. Take his size, for example. Everything about a fully grown Bernese is big and strong, massive and mighty; his body, his paws, his teeth, his tongue, his tail, his emotions, his responses, his will, his good, and, when they exist, not-so-good habits. Anyone who wants to adopt a Berner needs to think large. A Berner cannot be carried to the vet's in a basket; a struggling Berner cannot be pulled along on a leash; a fully-grown Bernese cannot be forced into a down position by the use of a hand—or even two. A Berner cannot be bathed in a sink, scooped up with an arm, or lifted across a puddle. A Berner slurps water with a bigger tongue from a bigger bowl (and thus slobbers more water on his folks); his coat takes longer to brush; he must go for longer walks. A Berner's paw leaves bigger, deeper, muddier tracks in the house, in flowerbeds, in the car, and on clothes; he shakes off more water upon entering the house after a hike in the rain; his tail wags with greater strength at a higher level; he barks less frequently, but louder. A Berner bounces more merrily, mourns more deeply, sulks more sadly, resists more strongly, clings more closely, and loves more intensely. A Berner *Sennenhund* requires more than the little finger. He needs the whole hand, no, both hands; no, still not enough. A Berner needs the total person.

Bernese Mountain Dogs are extremely people-oriented. In that respect they are truly high maintenance dogs. They crave close and—especially as "only" dogs—preferably permanent contact with their humans. That does not mean that a Bernese needs, nor should he receive, constant attention from his folks. What it does mean is that he wants to be a part of the family, to feel his humans' presence, to share their life. Anyone not willing to share their home with a dog should not get a Bernese. By the same token, a house where the dog is left alone, day in and day out, from morning to night, while his humans are out working cannot be considered a home for a Berner. A kennel run is, of course, completely out of the question. In fact, any confinement that serves only the convenience of humans or the safety of furniture and flowerbeds is unacceptable for a Berner. Putting a Berner on a chain is an abominable crime. People whose lifestyles do not welcome the presence of a large dog, people for whom surfing, sailing, sunbathing on hot beaches, skiing weekends, museum visits, elegant dining, overseas holidays, and similar pastimes are very important should refrain from adopting a Berner *Senn*.

While the typical Bernese is not exactly lethargic, he is not particularly active either. He does not normally chase around the yard, dash through fields, or become wildly enthusiastic about retrieving a ball or a stick. A Berner's preferred activity is lounging near the house, watching the world go by. This means that he needs to be moved regularly and extensively. A large yard is not a substitute for regular exercise. An evening walk around the block on a flexi-lead and a weekend visit to the dog park is most emphatically not adequate exercise for a Bernese Mountain Dog. Rain or shine, two one-hour off-leash walks daily, along with other forms of active exercise, are the absolute minimum. Anyone who is unwilling or unable to provide that should not have a Berner.

A Bernese Mountain Dog is big and strong. He may not eat as much as those unfamiliar with the breed would assume. Still, one must realistically anticipate that a Berner needs a larger amount of high-quality food than does a little dog. The cost for this is substantial. If one adds to this the multitude of other fixed expenses (from bed to bowl, from tax to toys to training classes, from vitamins to vet visits), the total quickly approaches the cost of maintaining a small car. These expenses will increase exponentially if the dog should experience severe health problems.

The Berner's coat is luxurious, thick, and long. Bernese shed. A lot. And then some more. Maintaining the beauty of your Berner's coat requires regular, intensive brushing. Even if the dog is thoroughly groomed several times a week, there will always be Berner hair throughout the house; even the most scrupulous housekeeping cannot keep up with the constant dirt and dust a Berner brings with him. Anyone unwilling to accept that, in a Berner household, Berner hair is a standard ingredient in food and drinks should realize that a Berner is not for him or her.

Something else must be addressed here. Although all puppies are cute, a baby Berner is the ultimate in cuteness and cuddliness. Each and every Berner pup is drop-dead adorable. Anybody

THE BERNESE MOUNTAIN DOG

will be enraptured at the sight of one of those tri-colored, soft, velvety, chubby, roly-poly balls of fur. His bear-cub-like movements are clumsy yet nimble; his dark eyes shine and his pink tongue shimmers. The grown-up Bernese also has the reputation of being an absolute softie; he is said to be extremely gentle, exceptionally friendly, especially good with children, and euphorically eager to learn. Too many people are therefore led to believe that the clumsy, darling fluff-ball, the playful bundle of joy, will automatically grow into the mighty, good-natured huggy-bear that is more and more often seen in television commercials, movies, and magazine ads. They mistakenly tend to neglect training their little Berner buddy, which carries severe consequences.

It must not be forgotten that a Bernese puppy is, first and foremost, what it is by nature—a dog. As the enchanting little Berner matures and his individuality and personality develops, he begins to seek his place and to define his role within his immediate social environment, canine and/or human, pack and/or family. At the same time he will grow by leaps and bounds into a big, powerful, self-confident dog. Anyone who neglects to train his Berner puppy will later fight an uphill battle. Before you know it, the dog may be too big, too strong, too fast, and too dominant for you to handle. Now it will be difficult, and in many cases too late, to start solving behavior problems. There are legendary examples of a Berner *Sennenhund* seeing himself as master of the house, unmistakably demonstrating his dominance by curling his lips, growling, and even snapping at his folks. Or there are Berners who behave perfectly at home but are virtually uncontrollable outside. There are Bernese who pull so hard on the leash that they can only be taken out by a male body builder. Some Berners shiver and tremble fearfully at the veterinarian's; others are so aggressive that they have to be muzzled before the vet can touch them. However, no Berner is born that way. Not one displayed such unacceptable behavior the day his breeder tenderly and trustingly put him in the arms of his new partner. Each and every one has become what he is through the education and training he received from his human. There are people who allow their Berner to enjoy unlimited freedom as a youngster, then later try to teach him manners by jerking and dragging him across obedience-training fields. Whatever the cause of this human neglect of the dog—whether a well-meaning but mistaken concept of love, genuine and innocent ignorance, or simply indolence and laziness—this is not the way to educate a Bernese. It needs to be remembered that at the end of his first year, every Bernese, like every other dog, is what his human has made him.

The Bernese is an extremely sensitive dog, but he also experiences occasional bouts of stubbornness. In order to educate him successfully, his humans must possess two essential qualities: sensitivity and consistency. Anyone who does not possess sufficient compassion and understanding to guide the little bear onto the proper path, and/or who lacks the leadership to keep him on that path, should abstain from entering into a partnership with a Berner *Sennenhund* in the best interest of both partners.

People who are hectic or choleric, dishonest or arrogant, egocentric, narcissistic, cynical, megalomaniacal, or tyrannical are not to a Berner's liking. Nor are people who lack clear values and firm principles. If dogs could choose their own humans, there are more than a few people—including breeders and breed club officers—who would be without a Bernese.

And finally, the Bernese is a strikingly attractive dog. What's more, he carries that chic Swiss flair that smacks of Interlaken, Gstaad, Arosa, and St. Moritz. For more than a few people this is an additional, or perhaps the only, reason to acquire a Berner—as a trendy object of prestige, a status symbol. His attractive appearance and wonderful character have already caused the Bernese to gain an alarming degree of popularity. Many Berners end up with people who are neither willing nor able to provide them with an appropriate lifestyle. There are far too many Berners who are physically and mentally underchallenged, who are mere couch potatoes or—what's even worse by far—kennel prisoners. It must, therefore, be stated unmistakably that anyone who wishes to acquire a Bernese Mountain Dog mainly as an attractive accessory or a decorative addition to a stylish ambience will be better off with a stuffed version—and the real dog will be considerably happier, too.

You, however, who are willing to open yourself to the adventure of fully sharing your life with a Bernese Mountain Dog will be offered a unique chance to find happiness. You will find it in the eyes, in the warmth, and in the unconditional, lifelong love of this wonderful creature. Apropos of finding a Bernese, you will want to know where the breed originated, where and how to find your puppy, and how to shape, cherish, and preserve that happiness. The following chapters aim to answer these questions.

The **Berner Sennenhund** is named after Bern, the capital of Switzerland. Bern is situated in the Canton that bears the same name, on the River Aare, close to the Alps. The name Bern is derived from the bear, which is the city's heraldic animal. The bear pits in the center of the city are a famous attraction. Bern presents one of the most impressive examples of medieval European town architecture and is a UNESCO World Heritage Site.

Even in Bern, a pair of Bernese Mountain Dogs is a special attraction. This handsome male is enjoying the stunning panoramic view of the historic town center from the famous Rose Garden.

Later, he and his attractive girlfriend stop both crowds and traffic in the cobblestoned street in front of the world famous **Zytglogge** (Clock Tower), which dates back to the 12th century.

Bern

Chapter 2

The History of the Bernese Mountain Dog

THE HERITAGE

The Berner *Sennenhund* as we know him today—the dog bred
under this name according to a breed Standard—has existed for
one century. His original homeland is the Swiss Canton of
Bern, the valley of the Emme, the midlands around
the capital city of Bern, and the pre-Alpine regions to the south.
A distinct farming culture had existed in this area for centuries,
and the land featured many tiny hamlets and isolated farm houses.

Here, as in other parts of central Europe with a similar economic structure, farm dogs were
found in great numbers. According to recent findings (Bärtschi; Räber), the origin of those dogs
likely dates back to pre-Christian times. Their history was directly connected to the development of
the central European farming culture and lifestyle. Over the course of centuries, people living in this
region bred and raised farm and herding dogs that suited their needs and met the demands of their
everyday life. What then, were these dogs needed and used for? What skills and abilities were
required of them? What characteristics did their masters consider desirable?

Obviously, such a dog had to be very people-oriented and closely bonded with his folk. He had
to be absolutely loyal and faithful. He had to be a reliable guard of his and his family's home and
territory. He had to alert his people to the approach of anything unusual—including strangers—
with an impressive warning bark that varied according to the situation. In an emergency, he would
not hesitate to effectively protect his humans. This farmer's dog was expected to stay close to the
house without being chained. He was not to roam about, and he was not to chase, much less kill,
game. When away from home, he was expected to be a loyal and devoted companion. When
working in the fields, he was to stay nearby, yet out of the way, without having to be watched
constantly. The dog had to be an eager, skillful, and efficient help in driving and herding cattle, and

had to live in peaceful coexistence with the other farm animals. Occasionally he would be expected to pull a loaded cart or small wagon. In short, this farm dog had to be extremely versatile. He was expected to be companion, playmate, guard, protector, herder, drover, and drafter. Such obviously required specific character traits: intelligence, self-confidence, willingness to work, easy trainability, territoriality, loyalty, vigilance, fearlessness, imperturbability, and an even temperament. Physically, this dog needed to possess substantial size, strength, stamina, and agility. He needed a coat that provided effective protection against inclement weather, especially the winter cold. On top of all of that, the dog had to be uncomplicated and undemanding—healthy, robust, easy to feed, easy to care for, and easy to train.

It is not surprising that people other than farmers found such a versatile working dog useful. Soon these dogs were serving as companions and helpers to cattle traders, butchers, weavers, peddlers, dairymen, and *Sennen*. *Sennen* (singular: *Senn*) is the Swiss name for non-resident Alpine herdsmen who kept their cattle on mountain pastures during the summer, then brought them down to pass the winter under a farmhouse roof. The least important feature of a *Senn*'s dog (*Sennenhund*) was his looks. Beauty was not an essential requirement, and thus was not a

The Bernese is a versatile farm dog

Checking out an unexpected guest—with confidence

distinctive feature. The appearance of such dogs varied considerably. They were not uniform in size, and there was considerable variation in the texture, length, color, and markings of their coats. Some had long hair; others had a short double coat (*Stockhaar*). Not all of them showed the tri-colored markings that are a Standard feature of the breed today—some were black and tan, while others were red and white. Despite this variety, what they all had in common was their balanced physical structure, working versatility, and sterling character.

Until the beginning of the twentieth century, these dogs had no common name. They were customarily named for a particular marking. A dog with a blaze (German: *Blässe* or *Blesse*) between his eyes would be named *Blässi* or *Bläss*. If the blaze were narrow or missing altogether, giving the face a bear-like appearance, he would be called *Bäri* or *Bärri* (German: *Bär,* meaning bear). A dog with a white ring around his neck would be a *Ringgi*. Other common names were *Vieräugler* (four eyes), after the russet spots above the eyes, or *Gelbbäckler* (yellow cheeks), because of the patches on the cheeks.

While these farm dogs were a fairly common sight throughout the Bern region, there were also distinct local types. Dogs originating in a specific area or village could easily be identified by a common appearance. One such place was the hamlet of Dürrbach, located between Riggisberg and the Gurnigel Pass in the Schwarzenburger Land, a pre-Alpine area south of Bern.

Guarding the Senn's mountain cabin

The loyal and vigilant farmers' companion

There, the proprietor of the Dürrbach Inn bred such dogs for his own use and also to sell to others. Since these *Dürrbachhunde* (Dürrbach dogs) or *Dürrbächler* were of exceptional working quality and were particularly typey, they soon came to be considered ideal representatives of this type of farm dog, and consequently the name was applied to all their look-alike cousins.

The discovery

During the second half of the nineteenth century, Switzerland and other European countries witnessed a rising interest in purebred dogs, the art of breeding, pedigrees, genetic histories documented in stud books, and in dog shows, or—to use the German term for all of that— *Kynologie* (derived from the Greek *kuon*, meaning dog). In this atmosphere it was inevitable that the Dürrbächler, one of the typical Swiss dogs, would soon be of interest. At dog shows in 1902 and 1904, Dürrbächler were exhibited for the first time and in very small numbers. Because they were not yet officially recognized as a breed, they were entered in a special trial class. Four of the six dogs that were presented in Bern in 1904 (three males and one female) were later entered in the registry *Schweizerisches Hundestammbuch* (SHSB) of the Swiss Kennel Club (*Schweizerische Kynologische Gesellschaft* or SKG). Thus the existence of the breed was officially and formally recognized, and those four dogs became the foundation breeding stock of the modern Bernese Mountain Dog. The dogs were not registered under a kennel name, but—as was the custom at the time—by their call names: Prinz, Ringgi, Phylax, and Belline.

Two fortunate events subsequently helped to further the breed's development. First, a group of Dürrbächler fanciers formed in and around the town of Burgdorf, near Bern. These men—among them Max Schafroth, Gottfried Mumenthaler, Fritz Probst, Franz Schertenleib, and Dr. Adolf Scheidegger—shared a deep commitment to breeding and showing these dogs. The second—and decisive—factor was Professor Albert Heim's passionate interest in all four Swiss Sennenhund breeds (the other three are the *Appenzeller Sennenhund, Entlebucher Sennenhund,* and *Grosser Schweizer Sennenhund.* Those names have been translated to the following: Appenzell Cattle Dog, Entlebuch Cattle Dog, and Great Swiss Mountain Dog by the *Schweizerische Kynologische Gesellschaft* [SKG] and the *Fédération Cynologique Internationale* [FCI]). Heim, from Zürich, was a geologist by profession and also an enthusiastic dog fancier and cynologist. The Dürrbächler's excellent character and natural beauty inspired Heim's special attention, love, and support. As a respected show judge and influential author of canine literature, Heim was instrumental in securing the existence and promoting the future advancement of the ancient farm dog. It is appropriate to say that Albert Heim was the midwife of the breed and the mentor for the breeders of his time.

Valiant and stately protectors of their home

In 1907, Heim published a description of the breed in the official magazine of the Swiss Kennel Club. In the same year, the Burgdorf fanciers founded the Dürrbach Klub and defined a breed Standard, which was first published in 1908. After some debate, the club's name was changed in 1912 to *Berner-Sennenhund-Klub,* and shortly after that to its current name, *Schweizerischer Klub für Berner Sennenhunde* (KBS).

At the early Swiss shows, the number of Dürrbächler entries increased slowly but steadily. The breakthrough came in 1910 at a club specialty show in Burgdorf, which was held to gain an overview of the breed and the breeding stock available in the area. One hundred and seven dogs, an enormous entry in those days, were presented to the show judge, Prof. Heim. In that same year, the breed Standard was revised slightly. The Standard remained unchanged until 1951, when a few minor changes were made. Later revisions came in 1973, 1993, and 2003.

A comparison of the older versions of the Standard to the current rendering shows that the appearance of the Berner Sennenhund has undergone only a few changes. The modern Berner is

Home, sweet home

slightly taller at the withers than his ancestors were; the curly coat, which was originally quite common, is now considered a fault; the amount of white has been reduced overall, resulting in more balanced markings (before 1951 a white collar and a white patch at the back of the neck was explicitly desirable, and the 1951 Standard still welcomed a small white patch); and while deviations from the ideal temperament have always been treated as faults, the current (2003) Standard lists aggressiveness, anxiety, and distinct shyness as a disqualification before any faults of conformation.

Overall, however, the original Standard has not been significantly altered over the years. Today's Berner is the same dog Albert Heim championed and worked to preserve a century ago. Indeed, if one looks at the description of the breed in Heim's essay *Die Schweizer Sennenhunde* (1914), one would hardly find a reason why anything about this gorgeous dog should ever be changed. Heim stated: "It seems to me that the noble *Berner-Sennenhund,* through his perfect balance in every respect and his magnificent colors and markings, is really the most beautiful of all dogs. While many other breeds have particular features which make them interesting and beautiful and splendid, the *Berner-Sennenhund*—it seems to me—owes his beauty to his normalcy. There is nothing exaggerated about him, everything is harmonious, nothing is standing out, everything is in its natural place" (Heim, p. 38, this author's translation).

In that same essay Heim also described, with remarkable accuracy, the admirable character of the Berner Sennenhund. He wrote that "they are very attentive, they notice everything, they give evidence of highest intelligence and reflection, they are very animated and agile, they are very attached, affectionate, and loyal, and they are, as all Sennenhunde, without any deceit. They are bold and fearless, but no brawlers. All these are ingrained features of the breed, bred and passed on since ancient times" (Heim, p. 46, this author's translation).

A century later, Heim's enthusiastic description of the extraordinary beauty and admirable character of the breed has lost nothing of its validity. It is not surprising, therefore, that the Berner Sennenhund has become a national symbol of his home country. The Berner, or *Bäri* as the breed is often affectionately called, enjoys great popularity in Switzerland and particularly in the Canton of Bern, which derives its name from the bear and features it on its coat of arms. On the one hand, the Bernese Mountain Dog is widely held in high esteem as a loyal, reliable, versatile farm dog; on the other, his outstanding character and attractive appearance have gained him widespread popularity as a devoted and amiable family companion.

An affair with (welcome) consequences

For the sake of completeness, an event shall be reported here that occurred in 1948. A stately, athletic, and rather virile Newfoundland boy by the name of Pluto was long attracted to Christine, an absolutely charming and beautiful Berner girl who lived next door. Unfortunately, the two were separated by a fence. One day, Pluto caught a whiff of a seasonal smell so bewitching that it overwhelmed him with desire. He crossed both the wooden and the purebred barriers. Christine, the comely Berner girl, cast aside coyness and welcomed him with a flirtatious wag of her tail. The two got the ball rolling and the game ended in a tie. Love's labor was not lost, but yielded seven

Bernese visit
Bern

puppies—all of whom bore a striking resemblance to their Newfie dad.

In reputable breeders' circles, such a mishap would normally cause embarrassment and be hushed up. Not so in this case. It was a fortunate coincidence that, within the Swiss Berner club, an effort to expand and improve the breed's gene pool by adding something altogether new had been under consideration for some time. Such a step seemed called for as the breed had apparently developed undesirable traits in several areas, including temperament, movement, and coat. Therefore, an outcross with a Newfoundland had already been contemplated. Now that fate, via Pluto, had brought that idea to life, it was decided to make a virtue of necessity and use one of the love puppies to inaugurate a carefully designed breeding program. Babette was chosen for this historical role and was mated to a Berner boy named Aldo. One of their offspring, named in honor of her maternal grandmother, was Christine, a beautiful, typey, true Berneress. Christine was later bred to Berner Osi, and two puppies survived from that litter. One of them was Bella v. Angstorf, a female. The other one was—drum roll, please—Alex v. Angstorf. Alex became one of the top show winners of his time and a highly productive stud dog. Newfie Pluto's stunt has long been forgotten. No negative results were noticed; on the contrary, the experiment was acknowledged to have rendered the desired improvements.

As Swiss as
can be

Berners International

The popularity of the Berner Sennenhund did not remain limited to Switzerland for long. Only one year after the 1910 Burgdorf specialty show, the breed was introduced to Germany. Frank and Nanny Behrens, who had become acquainted with the breed through Prof. Heim, imported Senn v. Schlossgut, a male from the kennel of Franz Schertenleib, in 1911. In 1917, Regina v. Oberaargau, bred by Dr. Scheidegger, followed. These two dogs generated the breed in Germany. Their mating in 1919 produced the first litter to be registered outside of Switzerland, under the kennel name v. Sieberhaus.

In 1923, the *Schweizer Sennenhund-Verein für Deutschland* (SSV) was founded. The club represents all four Swiss Sennenhund breeds. In 1990, following the German unification, the SSV and the East German *Spezialzuchtgemeinschaft für Berner Sennenhunde* (SZG, founded in 1952) merged, retaining the name *Schweizer Sennenhund-Verein für Deutschland* (SSV). In 1992, a club which represents only Berners was established, the *Deutscher Club für Berner Sennenhunde* (DCBS). Over the years, Berners gained considerable popularity in Germany, as reflected by the number of dogs bred. In Germany, where dogs are not registered with the kennel club but rather with the breed clubs (each club maintains its own studbook and issues its own pedigrees), the SSV registered 192 litters with a total of 1,223 puppies; the DCBS registered 66 litters with a total of 389 puppies in 2002.

In Austria, Berners—along with the short-coated Sennenhund breeds—are catered to by the *Verein für Schweizer Sennenhunde in Österreich* (VSSÖ), which was established in 1961. That club registered 206 puppies in 2002.

In Switzerland, 107 litters with a total of 621 puppies, bred under the KBS, were entered in the stud book of the SKG in 2002.

Thus, in all of the FCI recognized Berner Clubs of German-speaking Europe, the total number of puppies registered in the year 2002 was 2,439, which just about equals the number of Bernese Mountain Dogs registered by the American Kennel Club (AKC) in the same period.

The Bernese Mountain Dog has also become increasingly popular all over Europe (Great Britain, the Netherlands, and the Scandinavian countries in particular), as well as overseas. Fanciers in the English-speaking world, most notably in the United States, Canada, Great Britain, and more recently Australia, New Zealand, and South Africa, have discovered a special love for the breed. In 1926, the first Berners were imported to the United States by Isaac Schiess. Recognition of the breed by the AKC came in 1937. The Bernese Mountain Dog Club of America (BMDCA) has represented the breed since 1968. In 2002, the AKC reported 715 litters and the registration of 2,567 dogs. In Canada, Berners are catered to by the Bernese Mountain Dog Club of Canada (BMDCC). In 2002, the Canadian Kennel Club (CKC) reported of 119 Berners registered. The breed was introduced in Great Britain in 1936, and the Bernese Mountain Dog Club of Great Britain (BMDCGB) was established in 1971. In 2002, a total of 769 Bernese were registered with that club.

Unfortunately, the current popularity of the breed has an ugly side. As a result of growing demand, more and more Berners are living a deplorable existence as breeding stock in the kennel runs of high-volume breeding operations. Worse yet, more and more Berner puppies are being produced by irresponsible and ignorant backyard breeders; more and more Berners are abused as whelping machines under abominable conditions in puppy mills; and more and more Berner puppies spend their formative early days not with their mother and littermates, but in a pet shop crate. Hopefully, the day will soon come when puppy mills are shunned by every culture and the pet shop sale of puppies is outlawed in every country on the globe.

The kennel clubs of most of the English-speaking countries are not members of the FCI. The system of breeding and showing in these countries differs in many ways from that in German-speaking Europe and other FCI member countries. In fact, the breed clubs/kennel clubs of several countries have each adopted their own Standard for the breed (see Appendix). It is especially noteworthy and commendable that Bernese fanciers and clubs in many countries are putting great effort into preserving the working abilities of the breed. An especially popular working activity is carting or drafting. Another interesting and laudable fact is the existence of breed-specific publications of remarkable quality in many countries. Thanks to the commitment and expertise of dedicated club members, Berner fanciers in these countries regularly receive expert information on such topics as breeding, raising, caring, feeding, training, showing, activities (e.g., carting, obedience, therapy work), and—especially important—health. The BMDCA's *The Alpenhorn*, the BMDCGB's *Magazine,* and the BMDCC's *Bernese Please* are noteworthy examples of such periodicals.

The advance of modern communication technologies has opened up an exciting new possibility for the exchange of information among Berner fanciers all over the world; it is a virtual Bernerdom unlimited. Various national and regional breed clubs, consortiums, individual breeders, and Berner-loving families and individuals have set up their own homepages on the World Wide Web. Many of these private Web sites are showcases of Berner fanciers' unique artistic talents. Other sites are of outstanding educational value for both the novice and the seasoned Berner person. They are packed with invaluable, up-to-date information on responsible dog husbandry, modern training methods, and breed-specific health issues. Several international Internet discussion groups have been established. Some of these mailing lists focus on topics of special interest, such as breeding, showing, natural feeding and health care; others are forums for the exchange of information and discussion for all Berner fanciers. The largest of these Internet communities is Berner-l. On this list, Berner-specific information is freely exchanged and a wide range of Berner-related topics are openly and competently discussed. A large number of experts—breeders, trainers, veterinarians, scientists, lawyers, and other professionals, as well as seasoned, devoted conventional Berner people— generously share their knowledge and experience for the benefit of the dogs. Newcomers to the breed are welcomed and mentored by the great Berner community. On this list, the ingenuity, artistic talents, administrative skills, and financial generosity of dedicated Berner lovers regularly come together to sponsor fund-raising projects for the general welfare of the breed, as well as the well-being of Berners in need of help, regardless of their pedigree and registry. Here, too, an abundance of emotion is shared; joy over the arrival of a new puppy, delight at a Berner boy's first leg lifting, wonder at the miracle of a Berner girl giving birth, pride at the completion of a championship or working title, concern over a change in a Berner's eating habits, laughter over a myriad of Berner antics, sorrow over a Berner's failing health, sadness when a beloved Berner companion crosses the rainbow bridge. Bernerdom is united via the World Wide Web.

A capital Berner

Dairy Drafting

The Berner's constitution, strength, stamina, intelligence, and good nature combine to make him particularly suitable for draft work. Thus, in addition to such farm chores as guarding the property and driving or herding cattle, Berners were traditionally used to pull loads on little carts or wagons. Dairy drafting was (and is) a demanding as well as

In Switzerland

rewarding task. Every morning and evening, rain or shine, the dogs had to haul the milk to the local cheesery. Although motorized vehicles made the task redundant for Berners, there are farmers who take pride in keeping this long-standing tradition alive—and their dogs love it. These two Berners (daughter, 5, left, and mother, 7), just as the pair on p. 34 (female, 8; male 5), eagerly await being harnessed to their cart every morning, then brace themselves against the chest bands and, with obvious joy, off they go to the dairy. The combined weight of four 50-liter milk cans and the cart is 250 kilograms (550 pounds).

Berners pulling decorated carts, accompanied by their humans in traditional costume, are a frequent sight at Swiss folk culture events and enjoy great popularity.

Some harnesses are plain leather, while others are embellished with brass ornaments; all, however, are sturdy and comfortable. On some Swiss farms, where dairy drafting is still a part of everyday life, Bernese puppies are familiarized with the cart and the job by accompanying their elders.

Chapter 3

The Bernese Mountain Dog Standard

THE NATURE AND FUNCTION OF THE STANDARD

A Standard is a document that provides a description of a breed—a catalog of its distinctive features and specific characteristics. It defines the identity of the breed and describes the ideal specimen. The Standard provides benchmarks for everything about a breed, ranging from general statements about the model dog's overall structure—shape, size, proportions, etc.—to specific details such as tail carriage, ear shape, eye color, position of teeth, pigmentation of nose, and other such traits.

While the Standard portrays the dog in a standing position, it also comments on aspects of his movement or gait. In addition to describing the physical appearance, the Standard also describes the desirable temperament, as well as the dog's typical attitude and behavior in specific situations and circumstances. Altogether, the Standard provides the essential description of the phenotype, i.e., a dog's visible, tangible, measurable presence.

Every breed Standard portrays an ideal type—a single, agreed upon model against which each individual dog is measured. This does not mean, of course, that the Standard is a rigid pattern which should (or could) be duplicated completely and down to the last detail. Rather, the Standard sets a frame within which deviations are acceptable to a certain degree and extent. Although the ideal may never be fully realized in any living, breathing, individual dog, it must remain the ultimate goal. Some features and traits are obviously of greater importance than others; accordingly, the Standard assigns priorities to traits and features. In other words, there are deviations from the desired ideal that are tolerated to a greater or lesser degree. The rate of tolerance is inversely proportional to the relative significance of the feature in question; that is, it depends on whether the

Parts of the body

1. skull
2. stop
3. muzzle
4. lips
5. neck
6. withers
7. back
8. croup
9. forechest
10. brisket
11. shoulder
12. point of shoulder
13. upper arm
14. elbow
15. forearm
16. carpus/wrist
17. metacarpus/pastern
18. foot/toes
19. hip
20. thigh
21. stifle/knee
22. tarsus/hock
23. metatarsus
24. rear of buttocks

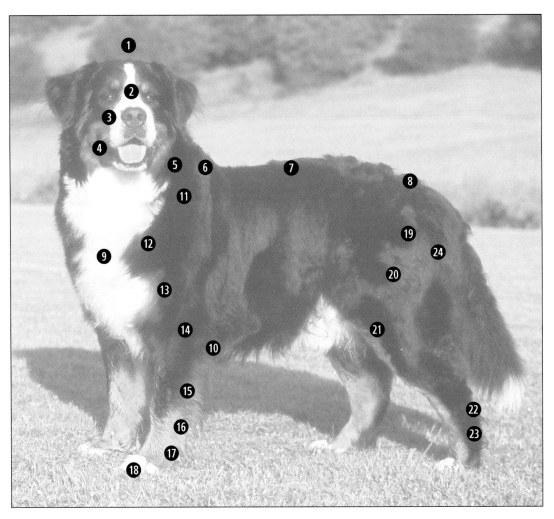

feature is considered more or less important. Obviously, and rightly so, those deviations—or, in the terminology of the Standard, those faults—that affect the dog's functioning (its soundness, health, and temperament) are of greater consequence than flaws that are merely aesthetic.

The statutes of the FCI provide that a breed Standard be defined by the national club of the breed's country of origin. In the case of the Berner Sennenhund, this means that this authority and responsibility resides in the KBS. Breed clubs are frequently accused of changing the Standard at will and without regard for their breed's nature and its specific needs; in the case of the Bernese Mountain Dog, such accusations would be unjustified. The original stature and character of this stately dog have largely been retained throughout its history as a purebred canine. The current FCI Standard is a product of the description that Albert Heim generated in 1907, which was based on the Swiss dogs as they existed at the beginning of the twentieth century. Since then, the Standard has been modified only rarely and with extreme care. The changes consist of little more than a slight increase in height and a reduction of excessive white markings.

The significance of the Standard for anyone setting out to breed dogs is obvious. Any serious breeder strives to co-create dogs that most closely approach the ideal type; in other words, dogs that are as perfect as possible in terms of soundness, temperament, health, longevity, working ability, and beauty. Breeding must aim to produce a dog that, as much as possible, represents the phenotypical characteristics described in the Standard while simultaneously reproducing those features genotypically (in the genetic makeup). The purpose of all serious breeding is to produce a dog in whom phenotype and genotype are identical or—simply put—a dog that is what it looks to be. The ultimate goal is the ideal Bernese who carries in his or her genes everything that he or she displays. The Standard, therefore, is the mandatory blueprint for every breeder and every breeding. It is the yardstick by which the success and failure of any breeding is measured and by which to assess the quality of any breeding program.

Dog shows are an important traditional form of quality assessment. At a show, the dog is evaluated by a breed specialist judge through comparison with the breed Standard. Therefore, anyone who considers exhibiting their dog will find it useful to be familiar with the Standard. The same goes for any potential puppy buyer who will, after all, want a Bernese who is representative of the breed. Only an educated buyer will be able to ask the necessary and appropriate questions, judge the quality of a breeder and her or his "product," and be able to make his decision with confidence.

The Swiss / FCI Standard

The original Standard for the Bernese Mountain Dog is in German. The following is the official English version as published by the FCI.

FCI-Standard N° 45 / 05.05.2003
Bernese Mountain Dog

(Berner Sennenhund, Dürrbächler)

Origin: Switzerland

Date of publication of the original valid standard: 25.03.2003.

Utilization:

Originally used as a guard-, draft- and cattle dog on farms in the Canton Bern, today also family dog and versatile working dog.

Classification F.C.I.:

Group 2   Pinscher and Schnauzer type-Molossoid breeds-Swiss Mountain and Cattle Dogs and other breeds.

Section 3   Swiss Cattle Dogs.
Without working trial.

Brief Historical Summary:

The Bernese Mountain Dog is a farm dog of ancestral origin which was used as a guard and draft dog and for driving cattle in the pre-Alpine regions and in the midland areas around Bern. Originally he was named "Dürrbächler" according to the name of the hamlet and of the inn of Dürrbach, near Riggisberg in the Canton Bern where these long-haired tricoloured farm dogs were

especially numerous. In 1902, 1904 and 1907, specimens of this breed had already been exhibited at dog shows, and in 1907 some breeders of the region of Burgdorf decided to promote the pure breeding of these dogs by founding the "Schweizerischer Dürrbach-Klub," and fixing the characteristic traits of the breed. In 1910, at a show in Burgdorf where many farmers of that region brought their Dürrbächler dogs, 107 specimens were shown. From that day onward this dog, renamed "Bernese Mountain Dog" following the example of the other breeds of Swiss Mountain Dogs, became rapidly appreciated all over Switzerland and in the neighbouring parts of Germany. Today the Bernese Mountain Dog is well known and appreciated all over the world as a family dog thanks to its striking tricoloured coat and its great adaptability.

General Appearance:

Longhaired, tricoloured, strong and agile working dog, of above medium size, with sturdily built limbs; harmonious and well balanced.

Important Proportions:

Height at withers: length of body (measured from the point of the shoulder to the point of the buttock) = 9:10, rather compact than elongated.

Ideal relation of height at withers : depth of chest = 2:1

Behaviour / Temperament:

Self-confident, attentive, vigilant, fearless in everyday situations; good-natured and devoted to his own people, self-assured and placid towards strangers; of medium and docile temperament.

Head:

Strong. In size balanced to general appearance, not too massive.

Cranial Region:

Skull: Viewed from the front and in profile little rounded. Frontal furrow hardly marked.

Stop: Well defined, but without being too pronounced.

Facial Region:

    Nose: Black.

    Muzzle: Strong, of medium length; nasal bridge straight.

    Lips: Close fitting; black.

    Jaws/Teeth: Strong, complete scissor bite (molars 3 [M3] are not taken into consideration). Pincer bite accepted.

    Eyes: Dark brown, almond-shaped, with close fitting eyelids. Neither too deep-set nor prominent. Loose eyelids are faulty.

    Ears: Medium-sized, set high, triangular in shape, slightly rounded at the tips, in repose hanging flat and close to the head. When alert, the rear part of the set-on is raised while the front edge of the ear remains close to the head.

Neck:

    Strong, muscular, of medium length.

Body:

Topline: From the neck running slightly downwards to the withers in a harmonious line, then running on straight and level.

Back: Firm, straight and level.

Loins: Broad and strong; seen from above slightly less broad than the chest.

Croup: Smoothly rounded.

Chest: Broad and deep, reaching to the elbows; forechest distinctly developed; ribcage of wide-oval section extending as well back as possible.

Underline/belly: Slightly rising from chest to hindquarters.

Tail:

Bushy, reaching at least to the hocks; hanging straight down when at rest; carried level with back or slightly above when moving.

Limbs:

Strong bones.

Forequarters:

Forelegs seen from the front straight and parallel, standing rather wide apart.

Shoulders: Shoulder blade long, strong and well laid back, forming a not too obtuse angle with the upper arm, well attached to the chest, well muscled.

Upper arm: Long, set oblique.

Elbows: Close fitting; neither turned in nor out.

Forearm: Strong, straight.

Pastern: Seen from the side almost upright, firm; seen from the front in straight line with the forearm.

Forefeet: Short, roundish; with well-knit, well-arched toes. Turned neither in nor out.

Hindquarters:

Seen from the rear straight and parallel, not too close.

Upper thigh: Long, broad, strong and well muscled.

Stifle: Distinctly well bent.

Lower thigh: Long and oblique.

Hock joint: Strong, well angulated.

Metatarsus: Set almost vertically. Dewclaws to be removed (except in those countries where it is prohibited by law).

Hind feet: Slightly less arched than forefeet, turned neither in nor out.

Gait / Movement:

Sound and balanced movement in all gaits covering a lot of ground; free stride reaching well out in front, with good drive from behind; at the trot, coming and going, legs moving forward in a straight line.

A majestic, mature head—
the Berner's crowning glory

Coat

Hair: Long, shining, straight or slightly wavy.

Colour: Jet black main colour with rich tan markings on the cheeks, above the eyes, on all four legs and on the chest, and with white markings as follows:

- Clean white symmetrical markings on the head: blaze extending towards the nose on both sides to a muzzle band; the blaze should not reach the tan markings above the eyes, and the white muzzle band should not extend beyond the corners of the mouth.
- Moderately broad, unbroken white marking on throat and chest.
- Desirable: white feet, white tip of tail.
- Tolerated: small white patch on nape of neck, small white anal patch.

Size:

Height at withers: for dogs: 64–70 cm

       ideal size: 66–68 cm

       for bitches: 58–66 cm

       ideal size: 60–63 cm

Faults:

Any departure from the foregoing points should be considered a fault and the seriousness with which the fault should be regarded should be in exact proportion to its degree.

- Unsure behaviour.
- Fine bones.
- Irregular set of the incisors provided that the bite remains correct.
- Absence of any other teeth than 2 PM1 (premolars 1); the M3 (molars 3) are not taken into consideration.
- Coat:
  - Distinctly curly coat.
  - Faults of colour and markings:
- Absence of white on head.
- Blaze too large and/or muzzle band reaching noticeably beyond the corners of the mouth
- White collar.
- Large white patch on nape of neck (maximum diameter more than 6 cm).
- White anal patch (maximum size 6 cm).
- White markings on forelegs reaching distinctly beyond half-way of pasterns ("boots").
- Disturbingly asymmetrical white markings on head and/or chest.
- Black ticks and stripes within the white on the chest.
- "Dirty" white (strong spots of pigmentation).
- Black coat with a touch of brown or red.

Eliminating Faults:

- Aggressive, anxious or distinctly shy.
- Split nose.

- Undershot or overshot mouth, wry mouth.
- One or two blue eyes (wall eye).
- Entropion, ectropion.
- Kinky tail, ring tail.
- Short coat, double coat (Stockhaar).
- Other than tricoloured coat.
- Other main colour than black.

Any dog clearly showing physical or behavioural abnormalities shall be disqualified.

N.B.:

Male animals should have two apparently normal testicles fully descended into the scrotum.

Annotations to the Standard:

General appearance

This passage defines the frame into which a mature Bernese Mountain Dog should fit—that is, the basic structure that he or she should possess. The description does allow for different types of physique. For example, Berners who possess either a heavier, bulkier, and more massive (but not

coarse or clumsy) build, or a somewhat lighter, trimmer, and more athletic (though not dainty, fine, or elegant) constitution are permitted. Of course, not all Berners can be expected to look the same; they are, after all, highly developed, complex natural beings who are individually distinct, not machine-manufactured products. What is important is proximity to the ideal, i.e., a dog who, overall, presents balanced, harmonious proportions. Sturdy limbs and appropriately thick bone structure play an important role here. Fine-boned legs do not fit the overall type of a Berner, nor can they provide the strength and the agility required by the body mass. When judging the appearance of a Berner, whether with a view for overall structure or anatomical detail, one should always consider sex-specific differences as well. Male dogs are not only taller, but are also typically bigger, wider, stronger, and heavier. Female dogs are correspondingly and distinctly feminine in appearance.

The phrase "above medium size" refers to the high and low ends of the height range that exists in purebred dogs (Irish Wolfhound—approximately 85 cm or 33.5 in.; Chihuahua—approximately 20 cm or 8 in.). Within this range, the Bernese Mountain Dog ranks above the middle. The Standard does not say anything about weight. It is implicit, however, that the weight of a dog should always be in balance with his size and overall structure. Thirty-five to 40 kg (80–90 lbs.) for females and 45 to 50 kg (100–110 lbs.) for males is a good rule of thumb. Do not mistake obesity

A model Berner in his prime (6 years)

for substance. For purposes of comparison, the breeding stock certified by the German DCBS in 2002 averaged exactly 50.28 kg (110 lbs.) for dogs and 40.08 kg (88 lbs.) for bitches.

The term "working dog" here does not mean a dog which has earned a working title within the FCI system (e.g., Schutzhund). Instead, the term refers to the general working ability of the Berner Senn, as well as his physical and mental capability to carry out the tasks that a multipurpose farm dog has traditionally been expected to perform. This is a dog that can work.

When judging the physical appearance of a Bernese, do not forget that this breed matures very slowly. Even if the dog's basic structure—the proportion of length to height, the circumference of bones—is complete after about 1 year, it takes at least 2 years (or even considerably longer in males and members of particularly slowly maturing breeding lines) before the dog is fully matured or "finished." Only then can he or she really be assessed. This is especially true for the skull. There are Berners whose head takes 3 years or more to develop fully. It is with good reason, then, that in Germany, 18 months (in Switzerland, 15 months) is the minimum age at which a Berner can be entered at a breed assessment (*Körung*) which is required for both sexes before they can be bred. For many Berners, it would undoubtedly be best if they were not presented for the breed assessment at the earliest possible date. Such an assessment report will quite often criticize a dog overall, or a certain part of its body (e.g., head, chest, back), that is not yet fully developed. Half a year later, that report would likely be much different.

Important proportions

This guideline must also be considered in tandem with the desired overall physical balance of the Bernese Mountain Dog. The dog should not be too long, as his trademark is his compact structure.

Height is measured from the withers (where neck and back meet—at the highest point of the shoulder) to the ground. Length is the distance between the forechest and the rear of the buttocks (the thickness of the coat does not count, of course). Other significant measurements regarding harmony of structure are the depth of the chest (the distance between the withers and the under side of the ribcage) and the chest circumference (again, taken at the withers). Both of these latter measurements are taken at the breed assessment of the Swiss KBS and German DCBS.

As is evident from assessment reports, the certified dogs exhibit, with very little variation, the ideal ratio of height to length; the chests could be a bit deeper. The male Berner pictured on p. 40, who passed both the Swiss and German breed assessments, demonstrates the ideal measurements: height 66 cm (26 in.), length 76 cm (30 in.), and depth of chest 33 cm (13 in.).

Behavior and Temperament

The English version of the Standard specifies a "medium and docile" temperament. This means that the dog should possess a balanced mixture of liveliness and calmness—he should be energetic without being hyperactive, and calm without being lethargic. The word "docile" refers to the dog's inclination to be easily led and trained. Docility or tractability is an important ancestral trait of the Berner Sennenhund; in fact, the original German text stipulates "good docility." It is this very quality that has, from olden times, made the Berner a superb working, family, and companion dog.

The term "situations of every day life" is relative, of course. The life of a farm dog is markedly different from that of a dog living in an urban or suburban environment. The important thing is that a Bernese Mountain Dog should master all situations that are relevant to his everyday life, in his immediate home and outdoor environment, with the greatest of ease. He should be able to cope effortlessly with experiences to which he is likely to be exposed, such as strange noises, movements, objects, and people (singly or in groups). Also, he should be only mildly disturbed by unfamiliar, unexpected situations, events, or encounters; given a brief time for reaction and adaptation, he should remain composed. It is important to note that the current Swiss Standard describes the Bernese as "placid" toward strangers. The Berner is a friendly dog. This, however, does not mean that he would not protect his people or his territory, if necessary.

Ordinary expectations of a Berner's temperament must be high and they must exceed those of any aspect of conformation—in temperament, the ideal should be the norm, particularly if the dog will be bred. Of course, the specific personality of the individual dog also has to be given fair consideration. Not every Berner will display the same behavior in every situation. Each dog's personality is the complex result of genetically disposed (inherited) and environmentally conditioned (acquired) factors. Regardless of such individual differences in temperament, however, there are two qualities of temperament that must be considered atypical in any Bernese and hence must under no circumstances be tolerated or justified: shyness and aggression.

It should also be mentioned that frequent and excessive barking is usually a symptom of a temperamental anomaly in a Berner. Normally and without a specific reason, a Bernese does not bark. His reasons for barking are, by nature and number, few: joy at his humans' return after an absence, the anticipation of an upcoming walk, excitement during a game, or as a warning (of or to a visitor or intruder, and hence of danger to his family or himself). Incidentally, the more self-assured the Berner and the more stable his temperament, the less he will perceive that he is threatened by anything or anyone, and, consequently, the less he will bark. A Bernese Mountain Dog who barks frequently and excessively is a not only a nuisance but also an anomaly—unless the dog is terminally bored, in which case barking may be a sad protest of neglect as well as an indictment of his humans.

Head

A Berner's head is, in proportion to the rest of his body, strong without being coarse. A head that is too massive is considered a fault, just as is one that is too light; additionally, a too-short muzzle is just as inappropriate as one that is too long and/or narrow. Although the skull is practically flat on top, it appears to be very gently curved both sideways and lengthwise, especially when the ears hang close to the head in repose. When the dog is alert, the ears are raised and brought forward a little, causing the skull line between them to form an almost straight horizontal line. The term "stop" (facial-cranial depression) denotes the curved transition between the muzzle (nasal bone) and skull (frontal bone). This curve should be neither too flat nor too steep—it should be well defined, but not exaggerated. The furrow, an indentation of the median line from the stop up to the center of the skull, should be only slightly pronounced. Of all Berner anatomy, the skull is the slowest to develop. It is generally impossible to accurately assess the size and shape of a female Berner's head until she is 2 years old, and in dogs it takes even longer. In fact, it is not unusual to have to wait 4 years to see a male Berner's head reach its full glory.

Nose

The word "nose" refers to the soft, hairless tip of the muzzle or the nose pad. The nose, along with the lips and the foot pads, is pink when the puppy is born. After a few days, the pigment will begin to darken. This blackening process is usually complete after about 2 months; the foot pads catch up a little later. In an adult Berner, incomplete pigmentation (pink spots on nose or lips) is considered a (minor) fault.

Jaws/Teeth

An adult dog's complete dentition consists of 42 teeth: 20 in the upper jaw, and 22 in the lower jaw. Each half of each jaw holds 3 incisors (I),1 canine (C), 4 premolars (P or, in German terminology, PM), and 2 (in the lower jaw, 3) molars (M). The last molars in the lower jaw (M3) are excluded from consideration when a dog's dentition is being judged. Also, the absence of one or both of the first tiny premolars (PM1) is tolerated. The absence of any other tooth, however, is rated a fault.

In a correct scissors bite, the upper incisors close like scissors over the lower incisors, and the outer side of the lower incisors touches the inner side of the upper incisors. Unequal growth of one of the jaws may lead to one of several incorrect bite forms. In a level bite (pincer bite), the top incisors meet the lower incisors edge to edge, like a pair of pliers. While this type of occlusion is tolerated, either of the following two forms of dental misalignment is considered a fault. In an undershot bite, the lower jaw is longer than the upper jaw, which causes the lower front teeth to overlap or project beyond the upper incisors; in the overshot bite, the upper jaw is longer and the upper incisors project beyond the lower front teeth, which results in a space between the respective inner and outer surfaces.

Distinctly masculine

Eyes

Here, as with other aspects of conformation, one must distinguish between aesthetics and function. The Standard considers a dark brown, almond-shaped eye with well-fitting eyelids ideal. An eye that is too light, yellowish, and piercing, like that of a bird of prey, is deemed unattractive; a round, protruding, bulging eye is equally undesirable in a Berner. Entropion, a condition in which one or both of the eyelids are turned inward, or ectropion (an "open" eye), in which the lower eyelid is everted, both constitute health problems and are thus faults of a more severe nature.

Ears

A faulty shape, set, or carriage of the ear is irrelevant in terms of function or health; however, such ears may disturb the physical harmony and expression of the dog's head and face. Thus, an ear that is too low-set (which is often the result of a distinctly rounded skull) is considered unsightly. Ears that are too long and heavy or are carried open and folded back are also a deviation from the Standard.

Chest

One of the essential functional aspects of a Berner's conformation is his powerful, broad chest, which should be equally well defined at the bottom (ribcage) as at the front (forechest). The shape of the chest not only affects the overall structural balance of the body but also the stance and movement of the front legs.

A ribcage that is too broad and barrel-shaped will often—especially in combination with deformities of the joints and ligaments—result in bowing of the front legs (elbows turned out and feet toed in). Conversely, a chest that is too narrow and has an insufficiently rounded ribcage will lead to an overly narrow, knock-kneed stance (elbows turned in and feet toed out, or "east-west"). A dog with either stance will automatically have unbalanced and orthopedically unsound movement.

Topline/Back

The back should "give" only slightly when pressed with the hand. It should be level—neither concave (sway back) nor convex (roach or camel back). Since the skeletal growth of the forequarters and the hindquarters typically progresses in asynchronous leaps, the rear of most Berners will, at one time or another, be higher than the front. In most cases, this unevenness will level out over time. Some Berners, however, will be high in the rear even after the completion of skeletal growth; their backline is then not horizontal but rises towards the croup. This phenomenon, which frequently occurs in combination with underangulation of the stifle (knee), may be optically emphasized in dogs whose coat, at the croup, is particularly wavy and therefore appears a little more voluminous. Under no circumstances should the backline (the line from the withers to the end of the croup) drop.

Underline/Belly

The underline should rise only gently from chest towards the rear in such a way that the belly is not tucked up.

Tail

A frequent and unsightly fault displayed by the Berner Sennenhund is a tail that is carried too high (gay tail) or curved over the back (sickle tail). Of course, the tail may go up when the dog is alert or excited—for instance, when meeting another dog. A clearly curled tail, even if not carried over the back, is also considered a fault, as is a kink tail, which is bent because of a deformity of the caudal vertebrae.

Distinctly feminine

Limbs

A straight and parallel stance, sufficient substance of bone, adequate angulation of the joints, strong ligaments, and well-defined muscles are absolutely necessary to ensure a Berner's orthopedic health and soundness of movement. It is only when all these factors combine and interact perfectly that unimpaired mobility is ensured. Any skeletal abnormality will result, sooner or later, in a disturbance of the dog's well-being and function.

Gait/Movement

The Berner's movement should be balanced and powerful, with good reach in all gaits (walk, trot, and gallop). The trot is the natural, comfortable, efficient gait of a working dog. Quite a few Berners, especially those that carry excessive weight or have insufficient rear angulation, show a tendency toward pacing, especially when moving downhill. In pacing, the feet are not advanced diagonally; instead, both legs on one side move in unison, followed by both legs on the opposite side. This lateral gait is not unusual when the dog is walking very slowly; when speed increases,

however, pacing is not only unaesthetic but highly inefficient and dysfunctional because it prevents both a free stride in front and a powerful drive from behind.

Dewclaws are the rudimentary fifth toes found on the inside of the rear legs. Since they are not only useless but also a hindrance (and a frequent cause of injuries), they are removed by a veterinarian a few days after birth. The front dewclaws are not mentioned in the Standard; they are left intact as a matter of course.

Coat

The Bernese Mountain Dog's coat is thick and long with a fine undercoat. Males generally have a longer and more profuse coat, particularly on the chest. Occasionally the skin under the neck and on the chest is especially ample; this results in a sideways, back-and-forth swinging which resembles a white bib. An abundance of thick hair at the back of the thighs (breeches) and fringes (feathers) at the back of the front legs and at the base of the ears is typical for a Berner. The hair on the skull, the earflaps, the face, and the front of the legs is short and smooth. The Berner coat comes in several textures: straight, varying degrees of waviness, or even curly. The curlier a coat is, the less typical (and less appealing) it is, and thus the closer it gets to being considered a fault.

Color

A Bernese Mountain Dog's tri-colored (black, white, and rust) coat is one of his distinctive features and an essential part of his identity. The placement of the colors and their quantitative distribution is largely defined by the Standard. It requires markings that are as perfectly symmetrical as possible and are proportionally balanced. Certain deviations, such as a somewhat lighter rust color, occasional dark-pigmented spots in the white noseband (freckles), a few black ticks in the rust on the feet (sooty or bleeding tan), a little white spot on the nape of the neck ("Swiss kiss"), a small white patch in the tan around the anal region (anal patch), and a few others, are tolerated. On the whole, however, and especially regarding the amount of white, the Standard is very restrictive.

It is difficult to accept that faults of marking should be accorded the same significance as are severe impediments of functional soundness, health, or temperament. However, because the balanced, symmetrical white markings are essential to the strikingly appealing looks of the Bernese Mountain Dog, it is highly possible that the importance of markings may be overemphasized. For example, a white cross on the chest, which was required by earlier versions of the Standard and which today is still sentimentally viewed by many as the "Swiss Cross" (reminiscent of the national flag of Switzerland), is considered a highly desirable feature by many. In this context, it is worthwhile to consider what Albert Heim wrote regarding markings: "Should size of markings and absolute symmetry of colors be a goal in breeding? No, three times no! We had much rather that one dog looks different from another, the one having a little more white, the other a little less. Uniform appearance of every dog should never be the ideal. Let us not take beauty to the point of boredom! A certain diversity within a defined framework should continue to exist. Soundness of structure and consistency of type are what matters most." (Heim, p. 39 ff; this author's translation).

Faults

The concept of the term "fault," as defined by the Standard, is to ensure that in assessing a dog, the critical evaluation of individual features should always be proportional to the overall appearance and relative to its constituent components. Thus, the total appearance of the dog should be considered, and care should be taken to avoid judging (either positively or negatively) a dog on the basis of one or several isolated individual features.

Eliminating faults

If a Berner Sennenhund who carries an eliminating fault is presented at a show or breed assessment, he or she will be given a disqualifying grade and hence cannot be bred under the FCI system.

N.B.

A male Bernese Mountain Dog who does not have two testicles descended into the scrotum may well be a perfect specimen of the breed in every other respect; however, a dog with such a condition (called unilateral or bilateral cryptorchidism) cannot be entered at shows nor at a breed assessment.

Chapter 4

Your Berner Puppy

**PURCHASING A PUPPY: TWO PRINCIPLES
'TIL DEATH DO US PART**

Anyone who adopts a Bernese puppy must wittingly and
willingly establish a lifetime partnership. Unlike a partnership
between two people in which both parties choose to make a
commitment, a partnership between human and dog is based on
a unilateral act of will. You choose to bring the dog into your life
in a state of utter dependence without asking the dog's consent.

You expect—or at least accept as a matter of course—that your dog-partner will give you
lifelong devotion and unconditional loyalty. The dog has every right to expect the same from you.
There are only very few exceptional reasons that would justify termination of this lifelong
partnership (or, to put it bluntly, getting rid of the dog) by the humans. A change of residence or job
is not a valid reason. Nor are behavioral problems (that most often result from inadequate training)
or health problems (which are always a risk) that arise in the dog. There are only three legitimate
reasons to part with a dog, and in each case expert counsel and a second opinion should be sought
before the ultimate action is taken. The reasons are:
- The human partner, due to illness or accident, is no longer able to adequately provide for the
  dog's well-being;
- The dog is so severely people-aggressive that rehabilitation does not seem possible;
- The dog's health has deteriorated to a point at which euthanasia becomes the final, necessary
  act of love.

Under normal circumstances, however, the condition "til death do us part" is sine qua non.

Investigate before you "take your vows"

The significance of this second principle follows naturally from the first. The inquiry that must be undertaken before one purchases a Bernese puppy focuses on four questions:

1. Do I really want a dog?
2. Do I really want a Bernese?
3. Where do I buy a Bernese puppy?
4. Which puppy is the right one for me?

Even if the prospective buyer, after thorough introspection and investigation, has answered the first two questions affirmatively, his work is not yet done. The answers to the last two questions also require considerable research. Before buying a new car or household appliance, one normally asks friends, colleagues, and neighbors for their recommendations; reads consumer reports and compares different models; and scrutinizes warranties and chooses a dealer with careful deliberation. Before getting a puppy, at least the same effort must be expended.

Breed clubs and breeding regulations

The previously-mentioned Berner clubs in German-speaking Europe are those recognized by their respective national kennel organization and, hence, also by the FCI and the AKC. Incidentally, only dogs having a pedigree issued by one of these organizations are eligible for registration by the AKC. Generally, any breeder who is a member of one of these clubs can be considered a safe source from which to buy a puppy. Such security, however, does not exist in countries where breed clubs do not exercise strict control over breeders, breeding, and breeding practices. Regardless of the country and cultural differences, the following rules always apply: never buy a Berner puppy at a pet shop, by mail order, via the Internet, at a puppy mill, from a broker, on sale, or from someone advertising "cute puppies—various breeds" in a newspaper. Never purchase a Berner puppy from a backyard breeder, even if the operation is a farm situated in the idyllic Swiss mountains. Never buy a Berner puppy at a kennel just because it is conveniently located. Regardless of the advantages that proximity offers, distance cannot be a decisive factor when choosing a breeder. Anyone looking for a canine lifemate for (hopefully) the next decade or so should be prepared to make a couple of weekend trips. Good breeders do not normally need to advertise; their puppies are usually spoken for well before they are born. Occasional ads for Berner pups in the canine press are the exception. Phrases such as "lovingly raised," "with papers," "pedigreed," "purebred," or "champion lines" do not mean anything at all. Anyone can issue their own pedigree for a dog; such documents are not worth the paper they are printed on. A pedigree is of value only if it reliably verifies a dog's ancestors, health clearances, and titles, if any (note: while health clearances are a must, titles are fairly rare—see chapter 7). It can safely be said that Berners bred under the auspices of one of the above named breed clubs will have a valid pedigree. The breeding of Bernese Mountain Dogs under all the recognized breed clubs is subject to strict quality control. For example, the clubs issue and enforce rigorous specifications (based on humane law and kennel club rules) regarding breeding, care, maintenance, kennel environment, exercise, socialization, and other such conditions under which dogs are bred and raised. The names of recognized Berner clubs with similar quality requirements in other European countries can be obtained from the kennel club of the respective country as listed on the FCI Web site. In Switzerland, a breeder can apply for a special quality seal (*Goldenes Gütezeichen*) which is awarded by the SKG if the kennel facilities meet particularly high standards. This award is then proudly and prominently displayed at the breeder's home.

...to play games
with its peers

One important element in maintaining and improving the breed is the careful selection of breeding stock. In German-speaking Europe (as in a number of other European countries), every Bernese Mountain Dog (male or female) intended for breeding must pass a Körung for both conformation and temperament. The assessment is conducted by a committee (*Körkommission*) of the respective breed club. In Germany, two of the three panel members must be specialist breed judges; in Switzerland, the conformation assessors are also breed specialists who are trained, examined, and certified by the breed club, then licensed by the kennel club to judge Berners. In that country, two judges are responsible for conformation and two for temperament. Temperament evaluators are also carefully trained and thoroughly examined before they are certified by their club. The conformation assessment typically focuses on some forty details specified in the Standard, which examine everything from head shape to tailset. Of course, all dogs are measured for height. A dog that is shorter or taller than the Standard allows or who has some other severe/disqualifying conformation or temperament fault will not be certified (cannot be bred). In some clubs length, the depth of chest, and chest circumference is also recorded.

Temperament evaluation criteria at a Swiss Körung include the dog's general disposition, relationship with his handler, attitude toward strangers, behavior in a group of people, response to unusual visual and acoustic stimuli, reaction to gunshots, threshold level of excitement, and how quickly the dog returns to a calm state. The conformation part typically takes about thirty minutes, the temperament test about the same amount of time. The test site is always an outdoor area, such as the grounds of a dog obedience club, a field bordered with trees, or a park. The Swiss temperament test consists of three parts. In the first part, the dog's behavior with a group of strangers is assessed. The two judges and about a dozen helpers (men, women, and children) move about on the field. The handler and unleashed dog must walk through the crowd. Obedience commands are not allowed; only an occasional "Come on!" is permitted. People cross the team's path, come from behind, pat the dog in passing, and wave their arms or hats at him. There may be someone with a cane, crutches, a bike, a baby carriage, or some similar distraction. At one point, everybody claps their hands. Later, the helpers form a corridor, standing in two lines, shoulder to shoulder, facing each other, about 4 feet apart. The dog must follow his handler through this human passageway twice. Next, the corridor is narrowed to approximately 2 feet, and again the dog must follow his human back and forth.

... and to interact with adult dogs

The next situation places the handler (standing) and the dog (sitting) at the center of a large circle formed by the helpers. First, the people walk toward the two at normal speed; the second time, they rush in on them. When the people are very close to the Berner and his human, the handler is asked to walk away and hide behind a tree while the dog—held gently by the collar by a helper—stays behind, surrounded by the strangers for a few moments, before he is released. The purpose of this exercise is to test how the dog behaves under stress without the reassuring presence of his human.

In the second part of the temperament test, the handler and dog must navigate an obstacle course with the dog off leash. Under the close scrutiny of the temperament judges, they walk first through a curtain of plastic streamers that is moved as they proceed. Next, they walk over a large plastic tarp that is pulled at and rustled while they are on it. Then a number of unexpected stimuli are presented to the Berner. Someone bangs a hammer against a piece of iron; another person steps from behind a tree and suddenly opens an umbrella against the dog; one assessor waves a huge

sheet of cloth at the dog and rattles a plastic box filled with pebbles; another toots a horn, rings a bell, throws a wooden crate in the dog's way, and rattles a sack filled with empty cans.

In the third and final part of the test, handler and dog have to walk across a field, side by side with the dog off leash and without heel commands, away from and then again toward a person holding a pistol. Going and coming, at a distance of 50 m (150 ft.), a shot is fired into the air. The dog is permitted to be startled, of course, but is expected to stay with his handler and calm down quickly.

All the test results are entered in a report; one copy goes to the dog's owner, the other remains with the club. This report also contains the evaluators' recommendations—or even requirements— regarding desirable or undesirable conformational or temperamental features that should be sought or avoided in a dog's breeding partner. Such comments may read: "watch overall substance and balanced gait;" "mind rear angulation and stance;" "correct ear set and tail carriage desired;" "watch flews;" "only for males with straight limbs and firm pasterns;" "not for bitches with toeing-out front feet." The year's complete test results (with a photograph of each dog) are published in the club's annual stud book (*Zuchtbuch*). At the German SSV assessment, a blood sample is collected from every dog in order to establish a genetic database which will constitute a major step toward better control of breed-specific hereditary diseases. Also, the DCBS requires that if a breeding-stock dog or bitch dies before the age of 8 years, a tissue sample must be submitted to an institute of veterinary pathology appointed by the club in order to determine the cause of death.

In 2002, the number of dogs assessed and certified (admitted to the breeding program) in all of German-speaking Europe was 181 (50 males, 131 females). The distribution by club was as follows: KBS 7/24; SSV 35/79; DCBS 8/20; and the VSSÖ 0/8. The minimum age for dogs and bitches at the breed assessment (and hence also for breeding) is 18 months (15 months in Switzerland). The requirements a dog must fulfill before it may be presented at the breed assessment differ slightly among the clubs. All clubs stipulate that the dog be x-rayed for hip and elbow dysplasia (see chapter 9). In Switzerland, a dog must have received a rating of very good (*Sehr gut*) or excellent (*Vorzüglich*) in the Junior or Open Class at a major breed specialty show before it can be registered for the assessment. In Germany, two such ratings are required. While one of these ratings may be earned in the Junior Class, where this is the best possible grade, the second one must be awarded in the Open Class (in which the Berner can be entered only after the age of 15 months). Certification will normally be for life, but may be revoked if a dog should develop a disqualifying fault or produce in their progeny a significant hereditary health problem later on. In Switzerland, Berner stud dogs are not allowed to sire more than ten litters annually. Considering the genetic nature of many breed-specific health problems and because of the excessive use of some studs (resulting in an undesirable limitation of the gene pool or leading to the spread of an hereditary disease, if the stud in question is a carrier), this measure might well serve as an example to other clubs.

While puppy millers and careless backyard breeders recklessly exploit bitches, abusing them as whelping machines, Bernese breed clubs safeguard females in this respect. According to the breeding regulations adhered to by all the previously-mentioned clubs, a female must have reached a minimum age (18 months in Germany, 15 months in Switzerland) before she may be bred. A bitch may whelp only one litter per calendar year with a minimum period of 10 months between litters. Furthermore, she may not be bred after the completion of her eighth year. After that, she rightly deserves to enjoy her golden years with her human family. (There is no age limit for studs.) In Germany, if a female Berner nurses more than eight puppies, she cannot be bred again until 18 (12, in Switzerland) months have passed. Occasionally, a breeder will choose to have extra puppies nursed by a foster mother (wet nurse) at a different kennel who happens to have a smaller litter at the same time.

Free whelping is considered essential for the welfare of the bitch and the breed. One club stipulates that a bitch that has had two consecutive Caesarean sections must not be bred again. Another club notes the birth of a puppy by C-section on its pedigree. Dogs delivered by C-section cannot be bred together. In this context, it must be mentioned that artificial insemination is hardly ever considered an option. In any case, it would require the permission of the club's breeding committee and would have to be performed by a veterinarian.

In order to more effectively fight hereditary diseases, particularly hip and elbow dysplasia, both the German SSV and the Swiss KBS have adopted a system called *Zuchtwertschätzung* (ZWS). This program collects as much phenotypical data as possible on each dog, its ancestors, siblings, and offspring, with the goal of eventually compiling enough valid genotypical information to reliably estimate a dog's "breeding value" (*Zuchtwert*). On the basis of available data, a dog is assigned an index figure for, say, hip dysplasia (HD), with the mean index for the breed being 100. The higher or lower the incidence of HD in a dog, the higher or lower its HD index will be. Two dogs can only be bred if the resulting mean score does not exceed 102 (e.g., a dog and a bitch with scores of 92 and 106, which total 198, is then divided by 2 yielding a score of 99, which permits breeding; a dog and a bitch with scores of 98 and 112, which total 210, is then divided by 2, yielding a score of 105, which does not permit breeding). This system will eventually include a variety of health and conformation features. All relevant data— health statistics, breed assessment reports, detailed litter information, estimated breeding value, etc.—are published in the respective club's annual Zuchtbuch. In German-speaking Europe, the incidence of health problems such as Progressive Retinal Atrophy (PRA), von Willebrand's Disease (vWD), or Sub-aortic Stenosis (SAS) is not considered sufficiently significant in Berners to warrant general, much less compulsory, screening for these conditions.

A puppy must be allowed to develop courage and strength…

Breed clubs contribute further to quality-oriented breeding through informing, educating, mentoring, and—where club rules permit—controlling their members in all aspects of the breeding of Berners. For example, one element of breed control involves the inspection of every litter by a club breed warden a few days after whelping and again when the pups are 7 or 8 weeks of age. The warden examines the puppies' condition (health, size, weight, markings, and appearance) and also monitors the kennel facilities, the breeder's dog husbandry, and the condition of the adult dogs. The warden records faults that will prevent a puppy's admission into the club's (and breeder's) breeding program (e.g., faulty dentition, entropion/ectropion, blue eye color, cryptorchidism, kink tail). These restrictions go on record in the club's stud book and also appear on the dog's pedigree. The breed warden also verifies that the puppies have received their compulsory initial vaccinations against distemper, hepatitis, leptospirosis, and parvovirus, which are required by the club/kennel club. According to club statutes, Berner puppies must not leave the kennel before they are 8 weeks of age (10 weeks in Switzerland), and they must have reached a minimum weight of 7 kg (15.5 lbs.) by that time. When leaving the breeder's home, every puppy will have been dewormed three times, vaccinated, and tattooed on the right ear flap (Germany) or microchipped (Switzerland). All of this information goes into the breed warden's final report, a copy of which stays with the breeder.

On the whole, the breed clubs in German-speaking Europe (just as in many other European countries) provide an important service in the maintenance and improvement of the breed's health, temperament, and conformation. One drawback of a system with so many rules and restrictions is that a breeder may not engage in health screening other than that stipulated by the club; as a result of the clubs' efforts, however, the buyer will receive a puppy that bears a valid stamp of approval and seal of quality. No distinction is made between "show" and "pet" quality pups. A puppy with a severe or disqualifying fault will be sold at a reduced price. Otherwise, a pup is a pup, and each one is worth the same amount of money, and that amount is basically the same with every club breeder.

...to roughhouse with its siblings

Regarding the genetic significance of longevity and vitality, a special event deserves mention here. Once a year, Switzerland holds a Vitality Contest for Canine Veterans (*Altersfrische-Wettbewerb*). This "contest," which draws entries from all of Switzerland, is open to every breed. There are three categories: one for dogs over 9 years of age, one for the 10 and 11 year-olds, and one for those over 12. Single Berners and Berner kennel groups enter in impressive numbers each year. At the event, the dog is first examined by a veterinarian who assesses his constitution and condition, then by a team of judges who evaluate the dog's behavior, his relationship with his human, his agility and playfulness, and his senses of sight, hearing, and smell (a hot dog serves as the test object first and as the reward afterwards). Such events are an ideal opportunity for breeders to display their accomplishments in meeting the essential goals of all dog breeding: health, temperament, vitality, and longevity. Beauty of conformation is not considered at this event—it would only be icing on the cake. These veterans' contests are pleasantly free of the hectic pace, pressure, competitiveness, and envy of other competitions. Participation is more important than winning. At the end of the day, all the dogs are winners, having demonstrated something more important than any conformation championship: to live to an old age in health, vitality, and dignity through the loving care of their humans.

...and to enjoy canine family companionship

Choosing your breeder

When searching for a responsible breeder, your first source of contacts in any country is the National or a regional Bernese breed club. Contact addresses can easily be obtained from the kennel club or through a quick search on the Internet. Some clubs maintain their own breeder or puppy referral service from which information about whelped or anticipated litters can be obtained at any time. The strict breeding regulations and their efficient control by the Berner clubs in German-speaking Europe (a similar system exists in other European countries) ensure a fairly uniform and high level of quality of both breeders and breedings. One can generally buy a puppy with confidence from any breeder who is active under the seal of one of these organizations. Still, differences do exist. Not all breeders share the same motives for breeding, breed-specific knowledge, expertise and experience in animal husbandry, care in raising their puppies, degree of interest in the puppies' future, competence in socializing their dogs, willingness to mentor prospective puppy owners, or readiness to support "their" puppy buyers throughout the lifetime of the dog. Prospective buyers are well advised not to purchase a puppy from a breeder simply because that breeder lives nearby and happens to have a litter at the time. It is always wise and acceptable to shop around.

Dog shows offer an excellent opportunity to gain a first impression of the breed, the breeders, and their dogs. Here you will meet knowledgeable and experienced Berner people who can be asked about any aspect of the breed and life with it. Here you can also gain an impression of the type of Berner that you like best. It is amazing what distinct family resemblances can be discovered if you look carefully. At a dog show, you can also watch how different breeders interact with their dogs. How does this person treat his dog? What kind of response does that person receive from her dog—trusting, devoted, enthusiastic, happy, and tail wagging, or indifferent, reserved, and timid, with ears folded back? Whose dog displays a relaxed, confident attitude when his teeth are checked by the judge? Which dog puts his tail between his legs? Whose dog is growling at others in the ring? At benched shows, which breeder leaves his dog in the box or crate all by himself for hours? Who answers questions openly and patiently? Who makes negative comments about another breeder or another dog? Who praises herself and her dogs to the skies? At dog shows, people clearly present not only their dogs, but also themselves.

It is also strongly recommended that, as a prospective puppy buyer, you visit several kennels, regardless of whether or not there are puppies in residence at the time. With many breeders, one has to put in a request for a puppy well in advance anyway. On such a visit you can gain an impression of the breeder, the dogs, and the kennel environment. In German-speaking Europe, the breeding of Berners is typically a hobby and a family affair involving all the members. There are no high volume Berner breeders. Very few breeders have more than two or three breedable dogs. Many, if not most, have only one breedable bitch. When visiting breeders, observe how they treat their dogs—do they regard them as companions or commodities? See if the adult dogs are kept in a barren yard or if they live in the house as members of the family; if the puppies are reared in a barn with human contact only at feeding time, or if they are kept in the house with constant attention from their family; if they have to spend all their time on a bare concrete floor or if they have access to a grassy exercise area; if they are confined to a puppy pen or if they have the opportunity to develop their physical and mental skills in a specially designed playground area with a variety of interesting, stimulating, challenging, and simultaneously educational toys, structures, and surfaces. On such a visit you can observe how the breeder lives with his or her dogs, how he treats them, what she feeds them, what care he gives them, and what activities she undertakes with them. You can see how well or poorly the adult dogs are socialized and trained. You can also learn how the breeder deals with dogs that are not, or are no longer, suitable for breeding. Don't be afraid to ask where the old dogs are. Hopefully the breeder has assumed the same lifetime commitment to his or her dogs that is expected of the puppy buyer. On the basis of all these observations, a potential buyer will be able to judge whether or not a breeder would be willing and able to give advice and practical help if questions or problems arise (and, rest assured, they will) after the puppy has joined his new family.

Prospective puppy buyers can (and should) also ask breeders about their breeding program. Why has the breeder chosen that stud for this bitch? What are his experiences with this and other breedings? Ask to see pedigrees, show critiques, assessment reports, and photo albums. What stories does the breeder tell about his dogs? What information does he have on his dogs' progeny regarding their health, temperament, and conformation? What has become of puppies from previous litters? What experiences have other buyers had with their dogs? How long did the breeder's former dogs live? What were the causes of death? For you and your dog, all this is a lot more meaningful than any number of show wins and championships. It is, after all, more important that your pup have ancestors that lived to a venerable age than that they became champions before they died an early death of some breed-specific disease. By asking all these questions, you will also learn something about the breeder's ethics and professionalism. You will see whether he has a profound understanding of such an undertaking, or if the litter came into being by accident, or to provide his children with playmates, or because he thinks that it is good for his bitch to be bred once, or to make some easy extra money.

If you visit several breeders with your eyes and ears open, you will soon decide whom you trust. It will be that breeder whom you eventually ask to entrust you with one of his precious puppies. Yes, that is correct; the decision to get a puppy does not depend on a potential buyer's decision alone. A puppy is not a piece of merchandise that anyone with sufficient funds can purchase. Someone who wants a Berner pup must be worthy of the breeder's faith and trust. He or she must accept, even expect, to be scrutinized by the breeder, questioned regarding motives, life circumstances and lifestyle (family, job, work schedule, home environment, leisure activities), previous experience with dogs, and overall suitability for that most singular dog—a Berner Sennenhund. In short, purchasing a puppy is a matter that involves bilateral trust. Anyone assuming the right to investigate several breeders in order to decide on one must grant that same right to the breeders. Hopefully, a breeder too has her own criteria by which she screens potential buyers and considers them worthy (or unworthy) of her trust. After all, she is not selling an industrial product that can be manufactured at will and replaced on a whim, but a living, breathing, loving being into whom she has put not only her financial interest, but also her heart. A breeder is

responsible for each and every one of her puppies; she is not responsible for their failure-free functioning or durability, but for their welfare. Therefore it is the breeder who decides into whose hands the puppy will be placed.

Choosing your puppy

One of the questions you must address before you start your search for that perfect puppy (although, if chosen with care, every puppy will be perfect for its human) is this: boy or girl? The significance of this question is largely overemphasized; some sex differences that are often claimed to exist do not, or are at least not as pronounced as they are said to be. The only really important consideration is that a bitch normally comes into season twice a year, and you need to determine how significant the accompanying symptoms are to you. When a bitch is in season, hormonally-caused changes occur in her body and consequently alter her behavior. The symptoms include a red discharge from the vulva, frequent urination (marking), restlessness, a strong interest in male dogs, aggression toward other bitches, increased independence, and a tendency to be less attentive to her human family. The bitch may become obstinate and somewhat difficult, and she will be enormously appealing to male dogs throughout her season, which can, admittedly, be a nuisance. If you want to spare yourself all this, you had best discuss spaying with your veterinarian.

Male dogs are bigger, heavier, and stronger than females. For some, this factor may be decisive in choosing whether to buy a male or female; for others, it is irrelevant. Owners of male Bernese must be aware that they will have to keep a special eye (and a leash) on their dog when—and as long as—a bitch in the neighborhood is in season. An unwanted pregnancy is not a reason for joy given the health risks, costs, and responsibilities that accompany it. Male dogs lift their legs: they urinate on the rose bush, the apple tree, at each and every corner, on trash cans and car wheels, on every molehill and blade of grass. Bitches piddle puddles. Not so many, maybe, but large ones. Thus, you must weigh your options: would you prefer dead leaves on the rosebush or yellow spots on the lawn? Overall, however, the question has little relevance.

Common knowledge holds that males tend to be obstinate, wild, stubborn, dominant, refractory, and, accordingly, difficult to manage; females are usually amiable, sweet, gentle, compliant, and submissive by nature, and are therefore easier to handle and to train than males. Of course, there is some truth in that—but only some. Bernese Mountain Dogs are genetically endowed with a balanced temperament and an amiable disposition. They are highly cooperative and eager to learn what their new mom or dad teaches them. They will willingly accept and respect their humans' authority, but only if that authority is built through love, respect, fairness, and consistency. Authority is not a result of physical force but of benevolent education. A dog's recognition of authority is independent of its sex. It may be true that males generally display a somewhat stronger tendency towards dominance than females, and it does make a difference if a male or a female Berner pulls on the leash—a difference of about thirty pounds. However, anyone who finds himself in such a situation has only himself to blame. One must nip such problems in the bud, not by jerking and dragging the dog, but by motivating, leading, and guiding him to appreciate what is expected of him for his own safety and welfare. At the time a Berner Sennenhund, male or female, needs to be taught to walk on a leash without pulling, his or her weight is a negligible factor.

The differences, then, between male and female Berners are really not all that big. The question boils down to the buyer's personal preference. Some people are more attracted by a dog that is bigger, stronger, sturdier, more massive, and more impressive—in a word masculine—over one that is slightly smaller, more petite, less mighty, and less powerful. However, once the die is cast and you have decided on a dog, the question is moot. Given the breed's basic size and structure, what really matters is only that it is a Berner.

At the time you visit "your" litter for the first time, the puppies will be perhaps only 1 or 2 weeks old. To the unskilled eye, they look very much alike at that age. One—and, for some, the only—obvious distinction is the markings. When judging markings, it should be remembered that the amount of white will not remain constant as the puppy grows. As the pup grows older and bigger, the white patches will diminish in proportion to body size. For example, a blaze that may,

The bond is sealed for life

early on, appear too widely spread across the pup's head will, later on, most likely be ideal. Conversely, a blaze that looks "perfect" on a puppy may turn out to be a mere thin strip of white by the time the head is fully grown. That cute white tip on the puppy's tail may be reduced to a few white hairs when the mature coat comes in. A small patch of white at the nape of the pup's neck or a thin, partial white collar will normally disappear completely after a few weeks or months. In short, the importance of puppy markings, especially an excess of white, is usually overemphasized by first-time buyers and novice breeders alike.

Pigmentation, similarly, is of minor importance. In young puppies, the nose and, to a lesser extent, the lips are not yet fully pigmented (not completely black). Remnants of the original pink color often remain. Such spots will usually disappear after a few months; if they persist, it is not a serious fault but a minor blemish.

When choosing a pup, there are much more important characteristics to consider than markings and pigmentation. Substance of body, thickness of bone, size of feet, shape of head, completeness of dentition, correctness of bite, and the shape of eyelids are all critical features. A fine-boned puppy will not turn into a sturdy-limbed dog later on. A steep stop is not likely to flatten. A lower jaw that projects beyond the upper jaw is not going to recede completely and turn into a good bite. A lower eyelid that is now clearly sagging may—as the head grows—become a little tighter but will probably never fit closely. Eye color (unless it is the rare, disqualifying light blue) cannot be accurately predicted at this age. Puppy eyes are a shimmery dark blue. If you look carefully at several pups, you may discover slightly different shades; the deeper the blue sheen, the darker the eyes will be later on.

A puppy's stance and gait can be judged only with utmost caution. However, many severe anomalies are visible at a very young age. For example, rear feet that, at 8 weeks, are clearly toeing out will probably always do so. An experienced breeder who conscientiously tracks his puppies' development will acquire an eye for such things. He is better able to predict a puppy's future conformation than will someone who has only produced one litter on the side. However, even longtime experience is no guarantee that a breeder can pick from a litter the puppy that will become the most beautiful adult dog. There are countless examples of seasoned and well-versed breeders who are constantly searching for a first-class puppy they might later be able to use as a brood bitch or a stud dog. They critically assess with expert eyes, they look, feel, measure, weigh, compare, study pedigrees, and seek advice from other experts. The result? Six months or a year later the dog may be placed with someone else because it developed a fault that disqualified it for the breeding program. If it were so easy to predict a winner, if, by looking at a puppy's face, one could determine whether or not it is champion material, every breeder would have a host of champions at home. You, however, as a normal first-time puppy buyer, will not (yet) have set your sights on showing, much less breeding. Your desire is to get a "normal" puppy—and you will find that puppy in your litter.

When choosing a puppy, behavioral aspects are more important than any feature of conformation. A pup's behavior in certain situations may reveal essential traits of its character and temperament. If you take the time (as you should) to watch the puppies repeatedly and for increasing periods of time—playing with each other, reacting to toys, competing at the food bowl, being brushed, doing nothing, interacting with the breeders, the breeders' children, and yourself—you will be able to perceive certain differences. One puppy is lively, the next one less so; one is sluggish, another just calm; a third is fiery, and the last one hyperactive. When scuffling with each other, one will be first to give up and retreat; another always wants to have the last word or, rather, the last triumphant smack of a paw. While pup number one contently watches number two chewing on a toy, number three comes from behind and snatches it. One fluffy cub sits in a corner with a half-pensive, half-dreamy expression on his face, as if pondering the deeper meaning of Bernese existence; another ball of fur is struggling but determined to climb the wall of the playbox. One will allow nothing and no one (certainly not his siblings) to stop him from being the first to the milk bowl; another follows, padding along leisurely. One freezes at the sound of a popping paper bag, then hastily retreats into a corner where he stays until the coast is clear again; the next pauses briefly, cocks his ears, raises an astonished eyebrow, then continues unperturbed with whatever had been occupying his attention; yet another comes running, cocksure and curious, determined to get to the bottom of the thing. When lifted up, pup A wriggles and struggles to get away as if his life were at stake; puppy B relaxes confidently into human arms. At the approach of visitors, one Berner boy continues dozing with dreamy, half-closed eyes, while his sister comes galloping from afar to welcome the guests and check them out. Each of these behaviors is normal, and each is an expression of individuality. Each puppy has his or her own unique character. The question is, which Berner personality matches which human personality best?

Most experts recommend that the novice buyer avoid choosing a puppy that shows extreme behavior traits—to steer clear of the excessively rambunctious and the overly reserved—and select instead a pup with a middling temperament. An experienced breeder will be able and happy to guide a potential buyer in making the perfect match. In the end, however, personal preference is (and must be) the decisive factor when it comes to selecting your puppy. The first time anyone sees a 4 week old litter of Bernese puppies, they will be enchanted by their irrepressible, bouncy charm and delightful cuddliness. All seem equally fluffy, furry, funny, and frolicsome; there is no way to say which is the cutest, the dearest, the most appealing. At each additional visit, however, these cuddle-balls will have grown not only in body, but also in mind and spirit, which allows a careful observer to glimpse their distinctly different personalities. Sooner or later you will catch yourself taking a special liking to one of the irresistible little bears, regardless of any conformation criteria. That puppy now has her little paw in the door to your heart. She is the one you will look at and touch more often and more tenderly than the rest. And after a while it seems (is it illusion or reality?) as though this little charmer comes to you more and more often, seeking your closeness and warmth. The decision has been made. Next weekend you will visit not the entire litter, but your puppy, and you will whisper the name you have chosen for her in her little ear: "Bella!" And the breeder who has an eye and an appreciation for the wonder of mutual love will be happy to give his blessing to the selection Bella has made.

What does the future hold for this little one?

The farewell

The time has come for puppy Bella's first, and hopefully last, good-bye. On the agreed date and time, her adoptive parents are coming to pick her up. The breeder has given Bella an especially careful and loving brushing to spruce her up for the occasion. The new owners verify one last time that the little one is in good condition by checking her bite, feeling her navel, and generally looking her over. A navel hernia, if not too big, will normally heal itself; in severe cases, however, the breeder will no doubt guarantee payment for surgery at a later date. The breeder will, of course, present the club breed warden's final report. Normally, a written contract will be signed. In German-speaking Europe, the typical contract (often a standard form provided by the club) is very simple and short. It normally does not contain any further obligations or restrictions such as co-ownership, showing, breeding, or spaying/neutering requirements. One should be glad and grateful that, in such a contract, the breeder wants to reserve the first option to take or buy Bella back in case she—at any time during her life—may need a new home for compelling reasons. One should also happily accept the obligation to have Bella x-rayed at a later date for hip and elbow dysplasia. Additionally, one should cheerfully comply with the breeder's request to be kept updated on Bella's health and temperament.

At the time Bella leaves her birth home—which will typically be between 8 (Germany) and 10 (Switzerland) weeks of age—she is clean, dewormed, vaccinated, and apparently healthy. Although she is not yet housetrained, she will no longer soil her own nest. She is used to being combed, brushed, and rubbed down. She knows the feeling of wearing a collar; she has heard the sound of a vacuum; she has been touched by people; she has been on car rides. Up to this moment, little Berner Bella has been given the best possible affection, nutrition, health care, environment, and education and socialization. More can neither be accomplished by nor expected of a conscientious breeder, or covered by his or her liability. Your breeder has met the high standards of quality control, good breeding practice, and health care required by the breed club—or, where such compulsory requirements do not exist, he or she has done all the things that are considered good practice among ethical, responsible breeders in your country (e.g., health screening). One simply cannot hold such a breeder responsible for any health deficits or behavioral problems that may arise later in a puppy's life, unless, of course, he or she has willfully deceived the buyer about a preexisting condition. If a technical product is found to be faulty, the customer is entitled to complain and be indemnified; a puppy, however, is purchased "as is." If Bella develops elbow dysplasia after 6 months, is found to have hip dysplasia after a year, develops entropion, tears a cruciate ligament, dies of kidney failure at age 2 or of leukemia at age 4, is people-shy 5 months later or is aggressive to her human 15 months later, it is a matter of common sense that the breeder cannot be held responsible or liable for any of this, even if the courts take a different stand. It is this writer's belief that, pending the family veterinarian's health check, responsibility and liability for the puppy's condition, development, and fate shifts from the breeder to the buyer the moment the breeder kisses the puppy goodbye and puts her into the eager arms of her adoptive parents.

What never ends for the breeder, however, is his moral responsibility for the puppy's lifelong welfare. It is, perhaps, asking too much that the breeder keep an active eye on each puppy as long as they live; there may be cases in which a lack of cooperation on the buyer's side will make this impossible. If, however, it is brought to the breeder's attention that one of his puppies is in a serious predicament—neglected, abused, or in need of a new home for some unforeseen, compelling reason—then, morally, he must stand by his commitment. If for some reason the breeder is unable or unwilling to help, the stud owner is second in line to assume this responsibility. If both these parties fail, it becomes—in this author's firm opinion—the breed club's obligation to come to the rescue. Responsibility for the welfare of every single Berner belongs collectively to the entire club membership, not only (although first) to the individual breeder. This is even more true in the system that exists in German-speaking Europe, where every puppy who is registered, every owner who joins a club, and every dog who is entered at a show brings money into the club, thus ensuring that the club officers', breed wardens', and judges' work expenses are generously compensated. For Berner breed clubs in other countries (the USA, Canada, and Great Britain), it has long been a matter of course to spend considerable amounts of money and enormous amounts of time on a rescue system that helps to save and find new homes for dogs regardless of their origin, ancestry, or registration. Volunteer club representatives and other devoted Berner fanciers selflessly make their own time, talents, energy, and even money available to help Berners in need. They rescue Berners from animal shelters; save them from being euthanized; free them from the hands of careless, neglectful, abusive owners; and adopt or place them with new families. Even though the situation in some countries may be more critical than that in German-speaking Europe, there are Berners in need wherever Berners live. A breeder who does not participate in rescue activities has no right to co-create even one puppy; a breed club that does not rescue is guilty of abandoning the breed for which it claims stewardship

A Mother's pride

Going home

Little Bella will travel to her future and, hopefully, lifelong home on the back seat of the car, held in the arms of one of her new lifemates. Another possibility would be to put Bella in a crate (now and for future car rides). A towel will keep both seat cover and clothing dry in case of a minor accident. Longer trips require frequent comfort stops so the little one can relieve herself. Before opening and leaving the car at a rest area, put the pup on a leash. Once at home, Bella should first be given the opportunity to explore her new environment; she will soon tire herself out and sleep for a long time. When she opens her eyes again, a new life will begin—for her and for her humans.

Long before Bella's arrival, the necessary preparations have been made. Her humans have chosen a spot where she can rest during the day and a place for her to sleep at night. A comfy bed (a mattress or a thick, soft blanket, perhaps in a wicker basket) is waiting. There is a bowl for water and another for food (ceramic or stainless steel); a grooming case containing her comb, brush, tick tweezers, toothbrush, and curved scissors (which will later be used to trim the hair between her foot pads); and there are a few puppy-safe toys (say, a soft plush plaything, a rubber ring, and a ball). A small supply of food is on hand, and a place in the yard has been selected where she will relieve herself. Bella's humans have thought of everything; they have mended the fence, registered Bella with the town (dog tax), taken out liability insurance for her, made arrangements with the butcher for her diet, enrolled Bella in puppy kindergarten at the local training club, informed the veterinarian of the pup's arrival, and have perhaps taken out health insurance for her. Her humans have even made a will stipulating arrangements (including financial provisions) for Bella's welfare in the event that they should die first. They also have a book on canine health at hand, and have not only bought but also carefully read at least one guide on modern, humane, positive puppy training. Lastly, arrangements have been made for at least one adult member of the family to remain at home for the next few weeks to be Bella's companion, playmate, and teacher.

A word about the puppy's sleeping place: a Bernese Mountain Dog is a family member and, as such, Bella's place is inside the home. Ideally, she will sleep in the same room with her humans. That closeness will help her to get over the separation from her mother, siblings, and breeder. At the same time, it will make house training much easier. At the faintest movement or sound from the puppy, one can get up and take her to her designated spot. After a very short time, Bella will prove a perfectly quiet and very considerate roommate who easily adapts to her humans' sleeping habits.

Housetraining is easily accomplished during the day by keeping a constant eye on Bella and by taking her out after every nap, every meal, and at the faintest indication that she needs to relieve herself. She will have the run of the house and, with proper supervision, it will be only a matter of a few weeks until she can be trusted not to soil or be destructive—even when left alone for a couple of hours. In Europe, crates are not used for housetraining, sleeping, or as time-out quarters.

Just as important as her nighttime sleeping place is her daytime resting spot. Puppy Bella (and adult Bella) needs a sanctuary into which she can retreat whenever she feels like it. A niche or a den-like spot is best—she needs a place where she can be somewhat secluded, yet not excluded. Even when sleeping, Bella, like every Berner, wants to be close to her humans. If she should later select a different place, she will be allowed to do so. Depending on the interior of your house, it may be necessary to block an open door, passageway, or staircase with a baby gate early on. Uncoated ceramic tile or hard wood is probably the most practical material for indoor flooring. Although Bella will love the coolness of stone tiles, lying on a terrace in cold weather for extended periods of time will not be good for her joints.

During the first few months, and especially for periods of training and practice, Bella will wear a simple, flat, leather-buckle collar. The matching leather leash has a strong, practical snaplink. Bella will soon learn to walk on leash without pulling (a retractable lead is not a substitute for proper leash training). Wherever possible, she will be allowed to roam freely. Once she has successfully completed basic obedience training, Bella will get a genuine "Berner" collar (*Berner Halsband*). This round leather collar not only looks and feels good, it also slips on easily, is comfortable to wear, and—unlike buckle or chain link collars—it does not damage Bella's hair. Its simple style accentuates the natural beauty of the Berner's coat. Needless to say, the leash is always hooked in such a way that the choke function is disabled. Neither a pinch collar nor an electric shock collar is for Bella. Neither type of collar is considered humane canine neckwear in Europe. In fact, in Switzerland, the use of these devices is prohibited by law.

Berner Puppies

A Bernese puppy is the ultimate in cuteness, cuddliness, and charm. Every Berner puppy's face displays its own great personality. Once the innocent, trusting little bear is adopted, its existence depends entirely and solely on its new parents. Therefore, each puppy is entitled to lifelong commitment, loving care, and responsible guidance. Every Berner puppy is born with the potential and the right to become some human's dream dog; it is the human's responsibility to make that dream reality.

Berner Puppies

Bernese Mountain Dogs were originally farm dogs. One of the essential characteristics expected of these dogs is that they coexist amicably with other farm animals. On Swiss farms, even to the present day, Berner puppies are born into the community of cows, horses, goats, pigs, cats, chickens, and other creatures. Thus, they naturally develop the confidence and social skills necessary for successful interspecies interaction.

And Friends

A Berner Sennenhund will be unimpressed even by big animals, if introduced to them at a young age.

Early exposure to all kinds of living creatures plays an important part in developing the sterling Berner character.

Chapter 5

Your Adolescent Berner

Puppy Bella was the first to leave the place of her birth. Within the next two weeks, all her littermates will also go to their new homes, picked up by their new humans. The puppies, incidentally, all have first names starting with the letter *B*, just as the pups from the previous litter had names starting with an *A*, and those from the next litter will have *C*-names. The breeder usually allows the new parents to choose the first name for their puppy.

The puppy's full registered name will consist of its first name and the breeder's kennel affix (which in most cases is a reference to a place at or close to home, the name of a field, a region, a building, a vista point, or other such geographical marker). First name and family name are connected by a *v* or *vd,* meaning *of* or *from.* Of course, many Berners have a call name different from their registered first name.

One of Bella's brothers is named Mutz, which is a Swiss word for bear. Before Mutz joined his new family, his life was structured by the rhythm of sleeping, eating, running, and playing. The little fellow could sleep where, when, and for as long as he wished; food (or, rather, drink) was at first available at any time from mom, and was later provided by the breeder in generous frequency and quantity; there was space and time enough for Mutz to run about; and he could play to his heart's content with his siblings when and for as long as he liked. When Mutz was not sleeping, he was constantly learning. This learning took two forms. First, the puppy had new experiences every day in his physical environment. He got to know new objects, shapes, smells, and sounds; his horizons widened constantly. Second, Mutz learned appropriate social behavior through interaction with his mom and siblings and perhaps with other Berner relatives. He quickly came to realize that community life is governed by certain rules and the violation of those rules would result in unpleasant consequences. If, for example, Mutz disturbed his mother's sleep, pinched her with his tiny sharp teeth, or simply got on her nerves with his puppyish behavior, she—who normally was a model of love and patience—would curl her lips and give him a warning growl. If he continued, she would emphasize the lesson by whirling around at lightning speed and showing him her teeth. This would send him screaming. Mutz learned his lesson. His mother would never hold a grudge against her baby; the incident would damage neither his ego nor his trust in Mom; but he did learn to respect her authority. This natural educational process was expanded, varied, and intensified through contact with his breeder and other humans.

Puppy charm

The same activities—sleeping, eating, running, playing, learning—will continue to structure Mutz's life after he arrives at his new home and will have a decisive influence on his development. They will determine the growth of his body, mind, emotions, character, environmental experiences, interaction with his peers, relationship with his humans, and ability to function in their world. What puppy Mutz does not learn within the first few weeks and months, what his humans do not accomplish with and for him, what is not fully developed and established by the end of the first year, cannot (or can only with great difficulty) be acquired by the adolescent Mutz later on. Within the first year of his life, a Berner puppy must not only grow into a real dog, but into a real human's dog. Not only must he grow big and strong physically, he must also develop natural canine behaviors and skills and acquire the practical and social competence to live successfully in the canine world—in other words, become a normal dog. At the same time, he must learn to be the social partner of his humans and live comfortably within the structure of their world.

"Who says there's nothing good on TV?"

Sleeping

Sleep is important. Little Mutz must be allowed to sleep where, when, and for as long as he likes. His sleep is sacred; nothing and no one must disturb him. He is not to be awakened because he happens to be lying in someone's way, or because somebody wants to play with him. He should not even be patted while asleep. If, however, he is slumbering next to your lounge chair, it will do no harm to touch him softly, laying a gentle hand on his back, chest, or tummy. For a Berner, whatever his age, it is never unpleasant or tiresome to feel the physical closeness of his humans. While respecting the puppy's sleep is a must, this does not mean that absolute quiet is necessary. Normal household noises will not interrupt Mutz's dreams.

Eating

Eating is just as important as sleeping. If the adorable, chubby puppy is to grow into an impressive Bernese Mountain Dog, he needs optimal nutrition: food of first class quality, balanced composition, and sufficient quantity. Anything that Mutz misses nutritionally between the time he is adopted and the end of the main phase of his physical growth at approximately one year of age can never be compensated for later in his life. What Mutz is fed during the months ahead will determine his physical development, health, and future performance. Therefore, only the best is good enough for him.

In order to ease Mutz's adjustment to his new home, for the first few days he will be given the same type of food that the breeder gave him; his regular meal schedule will be observed as well. Later on, a new, individualized meal plan will be phased in. A Berner puppy is typically fed three times a day, although four meals are not out of the question.

Good quality commercial dog food is available in many varieties for dogs of all ages and dietary needs; such products are stated to contain everything a dog needs. If your Berner is fed a

A Berner puppy in his
natural element—snow

complete food of this type, no supplements should be added except those things which may be lacking in a processed food, such as digestive enzymes, essential fatty acids, and beneficial bacteria (probiotics) for intestinal health. The occasional addition of vegetables, either steamed or crushed, is fine. The addition of meat without bone will cause your pup's phosphorous levels to become too high and may overtax the kidneys; the addition of fat-soluble vitamins (A, D, E, and K) may cause toxicities when combined with pre-supplemented, industrially-produced foods. Individual minerals, such as calcium, given alone may cause an imbalance in the dog's system that can result in irregular, unhealthy growth and skeletal deformities. The addition of water-soluble vitamins such as B and C is considered safe. Although well meant, substantial food supplementation is likely to be counterproductive and result in an unhealthy acceleration of growth and weight. Young Mutz could grow too fast and put on too much weight during this critical period, which can stress the puppy's bones, joints, and ligaments and lead to serious orthopedic problems, especially with a dog that is very active or heavily exercised. When a homemade diet is preferred, its composition (protein, fat, carbohydrates, minerals, vitamins, trace elements) must be carefully balanced. The proportions of calcium and phosphorus are especially important. A typical home style meal should consist of two-thirds meat and bones and one-third grains and vegetables.

The following meal plan may be used as a basic guide for feeding a Bernese puppy: give him one dairy meal and two meaty meals per day. The dairy meal would consist of one cup of cereal mixed with a little low-fat cottage cheese and a cup of warm whole milk (preferably goat's milk, as it more closely resembles mother's milk), to which is added a little bit of calcium and a multi-vitamin and mineral product, the dosage of which is based on to the puppy's weight. Hearty bread can occasionally be used instead of cereal. The early meaty meals should contain approximately 150 gr or one-third lb. (later meals can increase the amounts to 200–250 gr or one-half lb.) of ground beef, some lightly cooked vegetables, a cup of cereal, and—again—calcium and vitamins. After about 6 months, take the milk meal off the menu and let Mutz enjoy two meat meals per day.

A fresh calf bone is a delicious, healthy treat for a Berner puppy

Discuss the serving of home-style food with your family veterinarian. Following her or his advice, one will feed the pup raw or cooked beef or poultry. Pork should never be fed raw, as it may transmit the fatal Aujeszky virus. The grains may now and then be replaced by rice or noodles. A time-honored delicacy for Berners of any age is fresh, green beef tripe or stomach. Soft calf bones or cartilage not only taste yummy to your pup, but also strengthen Mutz's puppy teeth and his masticatory muscles. The same can be achieved with a piece of hard, stale bread or—Mutz's favorite—a three-foot bully stick. Rawhide chews (which must not contain any additives) should never be given unsupervised because of the risk of choking or blockage of the intestines.

A Berner's diet should not be without a regular pinch of salt, an occasional spoonful of honey, and two or three raw egg yolks per week. The egg shell, ground finely, may be added. Raw or cooked non-flatulent vegetables (grated or blended) and fruit (chopped or pureed) are healthy and tasty additions. Modern nutritional science can hardly offer anything better to support bone growth than a spoonful of bone meal, fresh from the butcher's, added to a meal on a regular basis. And what would complement a freshly-prepared meal better than a grated carrot, some herbs (parsley, chives), powdered algae, wheat bran, cod-liver oil, cold-pressed thistle oil, a trace of garlic, half a banana, a cup of yogurt, kefir (or, where it is available, quark—a soft, creamy European cheese made from whole milk), a bit of fish, or a piece of cheese? (Mutz prefers Swiss cheese, of course!) In other words, your Berner's diet should be based on the human gourmet's principle—variety is the spice of life! If dinner always comes out of a can or bag, after a while it will no longer be as enjoyable, even if it bears a fancy label. Bernese are discriminating diners, and some are even more selective than their humans.

Feeding recommendations should never be taken as scripture, but as just what they are—recommendations. They must be adapted according to one's judgment, the dog's needs, and in conjunction with your vet. The only essential requirement is that, especially during the dog's first year, the diet provides optimal quality, balance, and quantity. Obviously, as Mutz grows, the amounts of food also have to increase. It is impossible, however, to state exact quantities, just as it is impossible to define an abstract dog's ideal weight. Both will depend very much on the individual Berner's build. The most reliable criterion to define Mutz's ideal weight and, accordingly, his food intake, is his appearance. A Bernese should never look thin or emaciated, even at the time of juvenile growth, when he will go through a phase of teenage lankiness. He should always look well-fed, though by no means obese. Of course, a visual assessment alone is not totally reliable. Sometimes a Berner's coat gives the illusion of a body larger than it actually is. A hands-on check will best reveal whether a puppy or adult dog is at a proper body weight.

An absolute no-no for Mutz is sweets. The same goes for overly spicy foods, which is why table scraps should not be a regular part of his diet. There is no reason, however, to withhold an occasional treat of leftover pasta, rice, or vegetables—even topped with a little gravy. On principle, though, nothing should come down from the table during human mealtimes. Also, food should never come straight from the fridge in order to avoid indigestion. A Berner Senn loves his daily routine. Therefore—and because it is better for the dog's digestion—regular mealtimes should be observed. Dinner should always be served at the same place, too. A Bernese will normally leave a clean bowl. Should anything be left, take it away. The dog should not be permitted to develop the habit of leaving the bowl half-full, then coming back later to finish the food. If Mutz is picky, let him skip a meal. In most cases, hunger is the best sauce. An obviously abnormal lack of appetite is, of course, a different matter. In such cases, the veterinarian must be consulted. A healthy Bernese Mountain Dog is normally a passionate eater; with him a spotless bowl is a matter of course. Needless to say, Mutz will never be disturbed while enjoying his dinner, and of course he has free access to fresh water at any time.

A puppy runs with joyful exuberance, but tires easily

Running—learning—playing

Physical exercise is absolutely essential for a Berner puppy. It helps to support and foster muscle growth and stabilize joints and ligaments; it strengthens the heart and lungs; and it is the basis for all physical performance and stamina. Too much exercise, however, is bad, and novice puppy people are often unaware of how little can be too much. Back at his breeder's place, Mutz mostly ran and romped with his brothers and sisters. They all had about the same strength, speed, and energy. When your little butterball grew tired, he would sit or lie down to rest, watch the others, or take a little nap. Now his litter mates have been replaced by humans, incredibly tall beings with incredibly long legs, who take giant steps and enjoy walking for hours. The eager little puppy wants to keep up with his new family, and he will follow them at every turn. And he will be so anxious not to fall behind that he will ignore or forget that he is becoming tired, and he will push himself beyond the limits he would have observed with his littermates. Even when his legs get wobbly and give way, he will continue to drag himself along. Only when his body fails him

completely will Mutz succumb to sheer exhaustion and plop down on the ground, wherever he may be. It is imperative that his humans do not allow this to happen.

A Berner puppy's physical ability must never be overtaxed. During the first days in his new home, exploratory walks in and around the house will be sufficient exercise for Mutz. Short distances are best: a trip to the yard to relieve himself, running after a ball, or from Mom to Dad and back, followed by a return to home base. No frequent climbing or (even worse) running down flights of stairs, no jumping off a table to the floor (or jumping from any height, for that matter), no hiking in the mountains, no jogging. As each day and week pass, one can expect a bit more of the little bear. Today, a five-minute sniff-stroll across a meadow; tomorrow, a car ride to the forest and a five-minute walk on a springy trail; the day after, a ten-minute stroll along a meandering creek. Two weeks later, Mutz will be ready for a slightly longer walk with a couple of two-minute intervals on leash between five-minute periods of unrestricted freedom. The following Saturday, at 12 weeks, he can experience his first short visit to town, then return straight home to bed. Mutz's excursions should increase successively in length and number until, by the age of 5 or 6 months, he is taking two daily walks of fifteen or twenty minutes each. By that time, periods of obedience training should have been added to his routine. Do not forget that mental exercises, like physical ones, demand considerable energy from your puppy.

A puppy develops self-confidence…

A Berner puppy needs a lot of exercise, and free exercise at will in a puppy-safe environment can certainly do him no harm. However, Mutz should never be lured or forced to overexert himself in terms of either duration or intensity. Many older Berners suffer from arthritis (inflammation of a joint) or arthrosis (a degenerative process which breaks down the cartilage). It is likely that, in many cases, these problems can be traced back to joint disorders that originated or were exacerbated by excessive exercise (often in combination with excessive nutrition) during the dog's first months of life. Even a yearling Bernese should not be subjected to too much exercise. Although Mutz may have reached his full height at 10 or 12 months and displays an impressive physique and good muscles, he is not yet fully developed. He will be 15 to 18 months of age before you can expect full-power performance from him.

What is true for the physical implications of running is also true for some other aspects of Mutz's activity. The little Berner pup does not run for running's sake, nor does he practice running in an effort to increase his stamina and speed. He runs for the pure joy of it and out of his curiosity to explore the world. Every walk around the garden, over the meadow and through the woods, is a huge learning experience for

…and appropriate social behavior through play with other dogs

Mutz. Every stroll is an adventure that brings him an abundance of new impressions, encounters, and experiences. His senses are challenged by novel smells, sights, sounds, shapes, materials, objects, and creatures; he is confronted with phenomena that may be friendly, strange, pleasant, or menacing. His visits to town offer new and totally different sorts of stimuli. All of these activities require a tremendous amount of physical and mental energy. Upon returning from a walk, Mutziputz will not only have a tired body, but also an exhausted mind. He needs to sort out all these new events—both consciously and subconsciously.

One needs only to watch the little one while he is dreaming to see him processing some of his new experiences. All of this should also be considered when deciding what and how much can be demanded of your puppy.

Another important factor in this context is play. When Mutz is playing—by himself, with other dogs of different breeds, sizes, and ages, in the park or in a field, or with his humans—it is important for his development. It boosts the puppy's self-confidence, strengthens the bond with his humans, and teaches Mutz to be considerate when interacting with his canine cousins. In short, play is education, but it is also exhausting. Every play period, therefore, must be followed by an extended rest period. Running, learning, and playing? Yes, by all means, but carefully measured.

Growing

Great food, lots of sleep, and plenty of exercise—all of this combined will, in due time, bear fruit. That 8 or 10 week-old cute, sweet, clumsy, vulnerable ball of fluff will, ten months later, have grown into a gorgeous, striking, big, powerful, agile, self-assured Berner Sennnenhund who is full of spunk, energy, and mischief. The difference is obvious not only to the eye, but also to the scales. The 10 kg (22 lb.) puppy is now 35 or 40 kg (80–90 lbs.). From the first day in his new home, Mutz begins to grow and thrive. One can almost see his body grow in height and length and width. The changes are not continuous and subtle, but rather come in leaps and bounds. One day the puppy is a little taller in the front, the following week a little higher in the rear. Now he is lacking in width, then in length. Sometimes the head appears too large, but, just a little later, too small. At one period the tail is too long; the following month it is the legs. Berners are quick to grow, but slow, oh so slow, to mature. While Mutz may have reached his full height and length at 12 months, in width and depth he is far from finished. That also goes, even more so, for the head. It takes at least 2 years, and in males even much longer, for a Bernese Mountain Dog to reach that pinnacle of stunning glory that causes people to stop and gasp in awe.

His dentition changes, too. Mutz will lose his 28 tiny milk teeth and grow 42 powerful adult teeth in their place. First, at about 4 months, the incisors come in, followed shortly after by the canines. A little later the tiny premolars and the first molars will appear; the huge and powerful lower molars emerge last. At approximately 8 months, his adult dentition should be complete.

His coat will also change in appearance and texture. The fluffy, downy teddy pelt of the early months is gradually replaced by teenage fur. For a time, the hair on Mutz's head will stand as erect as quills on a hedgehog. He will be Mutz, a.k.a. Muffin Head—just temporarily. At 4 or 5 months the hair gets longer and firmer, and becomes jet black and shiny. This is first noticeable on the ridge of the back and on the upper side of the tail. At about the same time the baby teeth are all out, the coat will be completely renewed as well. It will still lack length and density; the trousers at the thighs will look more like shorts and the feathers on the front legs will be hardly more than little fringes. With every seasonal change, however, the coat will approach perfection. At about 2 years (again, later in males) it will finally have attained the awesome beauty of maturity. In the meantime, Mutz will also have learned to bark and lift his leg. Both genders reach sexual maturity at about 8 or 9 months.

Obedience training strengthens
the Berner-human bond

After one year, Mutz is more or less grown-up, physically, mentally, and emotionally. Had he grown up without his humans, as a dog among dogs, he would now be a full-fledged member of canine society. However, his existence is not (or not only) that of a dog in a pack of dogs. Rather, he is destined to live with his humans and to share their world. If in the present and in the future their coexistence is to function smoothly and without conflict, by this time Mutzi must have learned the rules and behavioral norms that are valid in his hybrid world. Of course, he could not possibly have achieved that on his own; his humans played a responsible and decisive part in the process. They now must face this question: although they have provided their Berner darling with a soft bed, tasty and nutritious food, fancy toys, proper physical and mental exercise, and fun games to play, have they also assisted him in acquiring the social skills that are necessary for life in both the canine and the human worlds? In short, have they provided him with an adequate education?

Education for life

Education is more than obedience training. Education is both the prerequisite for, and the result of, a harmonious union between a Bernese Mountain Dog and his humans. There is no successful education without harmony, and no harmony without good education. This aspect of the partnership is eminently important. Education means making Mutz the junior partner in the human-dog relationship, and teaching him to accept that position gladly. Education is to subjugate the dog without breaking him, destroying his dignity, or making him a slave. Education, in this sense, does not seek to have the dog obey because he is forced to, but because he willingly and happily chooses to do so. Education does not aspire to produce a dog who is submissive out of fear, but rather one who is devoted to his humans and willing to please them. This goal can only be achieved through love, understanding, and responsibility. It requires an attitude of deeply felt and genuine respect for your Berner. This respect must be evident to the dog at all times. You must, at every moment, be predictable to your dog, because only then will the dog respect you and be predictable to you in every situation. Remember: respect begets respect.

To educate a Bernese Mountain Dog is to shape his temperament simultaneously and perpetually. Temperament, or character, is the sum of both inherited and acquired behavioral traits. The former have been bestowed on Mutz by birth; the latter are the cumulative result of all his experiences and encounters in and with the world. Acquired behavior is largely subject to the influence and the control of man. All character traits, both positive and negative, can be either reinforced or mitigated. A puppy born with the very best character potential can be spoiled by the influence of a negative environment and education. Conversely, inherited negative behavior can be largely compensated for through favorable circumstances and/or by deliberate and careful education.

When speaking of inherited temperament problems, one generally thinks of a tendency toward aggressive or fearful behavior. Both conditions (which are frequently different sides of the same coin) require thoughtful and consistent behavioral therapy. In some cases, common sense will suffice; in severe cases, the advice of an experienced dog trainer or canine behaviorist will be necessary. With Bernese, it is not uncommon for a certain timidity and spookiness to set in at about 4 to 6 months of age that may—especially with females—last well into the second year. Even dogs who, as puppies, displayed normal, confident, and outgoing behavior can be affected. Luckily, such a behavioral anomaly is usually only temporary. In any case, it is important to guide the dog through a carefully selected and consistent training program to strengthen its self-confidence and to stabilize its behavior. One occasionally hears of Berners, especially males, who show dominant-aggressive behavior towards their humans. Disobedience, growling, snapping, and/or biting the human family are always symptoms of a severe authority crisis. This is usually the result of either the human's authority not being firmly established at the appropriate time (during the phase in the puppy's development where his position within his peer group is normally established—around 4 months), or man's previously established authority being lost during the dog's rebellious phase of puberty (approximately 6 to 10 months).

Never too young for a visit to town

Education includes socialization. The development of a Berner's personality depends on the experiences he has with other animals—especially other dogs—and with people outside of his own family. Experiences cannot be taught, they must be lived; therefore, Mutz must be given ample opportunity, very early in life, to meet and interact with dogs of all breeds and all sizes without interference from his humans. Take the little guy up onto your arm at the approach of an adult Great Dane? Wrong. What is he to do when, later on, he can no longer be lifted up? Keep the puppy away from strange people, their voices, touches, smells? A bigger mistake cannot be made. Spare the baby the sight and sound of flapping awnings, rattling streetcars, screaming cheerleaders, or roaring trains? That is puppy love misunderstood. Lack of familiarity leads to distrust; distrust creates insecurity; and insecurity breeds aggressiveness. Temperamental stability requires confidence. Little Mutz can only develop confidence if he has a chance to experience his own strength by meeting new things and interacting with other beings.

The harmonious union of dog and man has a number of practical applications. The harmony is disturbed if, for example, Mutz pulls on the leash so violently that you lose your balance; if he jumps up on other people with muddy paws; if—on an off-leash walk—he takes off in the opposite direction; if he disobeys your request to drop a strange object that he has picked up from the ground; if, in a restaurant, he stares at your plate while drooling copiously; if he growlingly refuses to have his teeth checked by the veterinarian; if he protests against being left alone in the house with incessant screaming or destructive behavior; if the fluttering of a flag scares him so much that he jumps; or if he distrustfully evades the friendly approach of other people.

There are a number of behaviors that, upon request by his humans, an adult Bernese should perform reliably at any time, in any place, and in any situation. He should happily heel on and off leash; he should promptly sit, stand, or lie down; he should willingly stay in the sit or down position until called or collected; at a sound signal (call or whistle) he should immediately stop and stand; he should reliably come when called; he should release any object on command, even when he is at a distance from his human; he should remain alone without a problem in any environment (home, car, hotel room). In training a Berner puppy, force and physical abuse have no place—no yelling, no jerking, no dragging. There is a wealth of literature on positive obedience training. Every puppy buyer has the moral obligation to inform him- or herself through appropriate reading before taking a Berner baby home. It would be even better to study such information before deciding to get a dog.

It is imperative that a Bernese Mountain Dog be impeccably trained. His obedience (or disobedience) is, always and without excuse, the direct or indirect result of his humans' actions or inaction. Wrong or bad behavior in a dog invariably indicates some neglect, failure, carelessness, or incompetence on the humans' part. Dog owners tend to be quick to divert attention from their own responsibility. Comments like "normally he doesn't do that," "he only wants to play," "he was abused by his breeder," or "he was bitten by another dog when he was a puppy" are nothing but poor—and unacceptable—excuses. As Albert Heim correctly stated, "The dog is what his people have made of him; any negative behavior is more a reflection of the master's mistakes than it is a manifestation of an innate fault of the student." (Heim, p. 46; this author's translation).

A familiar expression about dog education is "what Mutzli doesn't learn, Mutz will learn only with difficulty, if at all." Any training must acknowledge that a dog's mind is most receptive to learning during the first 4 or 5 months. With Berners it is especially easy, as they are avid and quick learners, very sensitive, and only too happy to please their humans. They just need to be shown, with kindness and patience, what is expected of them. The puppy's education begins the moment he enters his new home. The first and most obvious lesson will be to take Mutz outside to relieve himself as soon as he wakes up. Immediately after he is done, praise him lavishly and give him a treat. Mutz will have to poop after every meal, so shortly after he has swallowed his last bite, take him out and repeat the rewards of praise and a treat. During his first days at home, one of Mutz's humans must keep an eye on him. Every minute. At the slightest indication that he is feeling the urge, take him out. In a week or two, the little fellow will no longer use the house as a bathroom (the occasional accident does not count).

No puppy, not even a Berner, likes to heel on leash. A puppy wants to ramble, stop, sniff, and run back and forth freely. The leash prevents him from doing so. The puppy will struggle, pull ahead, sit down, brace himself, and/or try to pull his head out of the collar. Don't wait until this happens. From the first second that Mutz is on leash, get his attention focused on you, your face, a toy in your hand, a treat in your pocket. Walk a short distance. Praise, praise, praise! Reward, treat! Stop. Take the leash off. Let the puppy run. Three minutes later, call him back. Praise! Cuddle! Treat! Put the leash back on. Walk a little. Praise, praise, praise! Reward, treat! Remember: leash breaking is out, leash training is in!

All training should be carefully apportioned. Mutz's attention span is short. Do not expect too much from a puppy too soon. Training sessions should be kept short. They should always be fun and should invariably end on a happy, positive note, with a "Well done! Good boy! Super Mutz!" For the puppy to learn successfully, you must maintain a calm and unhurried demeanor. If you have just returned home from a stressful day at work, have just quarreled with a neighbor, have just received an unpleasant tax assessment, or if you are just not in the mood, then you are not a suitable partner for your puppy's education at that time. In such a situation, a good walk will be better for both of you.

Patience is a must. Self-discipline is necessary, as well as the understanding that one always has to make absolutely clear to the dog what is expected of him. Training exercises must always and consistently be accompanied by the same words, the same tone of voice, and the same body language. Precision is important for both the human and the dog. Sloppy training leads to unreliable behavior. Close physical contact is important. The closer the body contact, the easier it is for the dog to respond to the stimuli given by his partner. These caveats apply to all aspects of training and education.

One thing cannot be emphasized enough: Mutz must be taught to submit himself confidently and happily to the hands of his humans in every situation. He must be brought to accept his humans' dominance as a given precisely because their physical superiority does not exist in reality. Don't forget that an adult Berner can outrun, outstruggle, outpull, and outbite any human at any time. Building trust while establishing leadership, authority, and benevolent dominance is important. A Berner puppy must be loved, hugged, petted, stroked, tickled, kissed, and caressed as often as possible, and for as long as possible. Glide your hand over Mutz's back, across his tummy, along his legs, down his tail; look into his ears, gently touch an eyelid, pat his head, feel his teeth, palpate his throat, finger his toes, rub his belly, massage his butt, and touch his tiny member. And then—for just a moment—roll him on his side or back and hold him still with a gentle hand while your voice sweetly soothes and praises him. A gourmet treat finds its way into his little mouth; it is a reward for the present and a promise for the future. In other words, now is the time to subdue the little bear both literally and physically. The invaluable fruits of this exercise are that, months later, mighty Mutz will happily lie down at a signal or the sight of a certain object associated with this situation, and will readily and patiently tolerate having his teeth brushed, a tick removed from his eyelid, the hair between his foot pads clipped, or his penis rinsed. A Bernese who is trained and educated in that manner will become a predictable, and therefore unproblematic, member of human society. Your neighbor's children, pedestrians, shoppers, waitresses, fellow passengers on public transportation, show judges, park rangers, mail carriers, veterinarians, and many more people will be grateful for your meticulous effort—and your impeccably trained dog.

The scent of the big, wide world

A Bernese Mountain Dog is a comrade for life, and for every day of it. Mutz is meant to be, and desires to be, his humans' companion for as long as he breathes. He should accompany them on all their journeys through their world. He should be a reliable partner in every possible situation, in every place, and in every respect. In order for him to be able to fill this role successfully, it is not enough to let him grow up in the security and freedom of the home and yard, field and forest. He must also be given the opportunity to sniff fully the scent of the big, wide world, whether it is the mouth-watering smell of a grilled sausage or the repulsive stench of exhaust fumes, whether sweet perfume or the sweat of strangers. In other words, little Mutz must, gradually and carefully, be introduced fully to the complex world of humans. Take him here today, somewhere else tomorrow. Quiet parks and bustling streets, county fairs and kindergartens, barber shops and birthday parties, boutiques and bookstores, toy shops and train stations, department stores and doughnut shops, hotels and hot dog stands, beer gardens and bus terminals, posh restaurants and pizza joints, carnivals and college campuses, ferry boats and cable cars, the seaside and mountain peaks. To experience all of this at his humans' side is not, as some might suspect, an unnecessary stress for Mutz; rather, it provides him with a wealth of world and life experiences, and it opens up an additional dimension in the partnership with his humans. A Berner who is thus seasoned will possess rich and versatile living skills that will prepare him well for any situation that life holds in store for him. Blessed is the Berner whose humans have provided him with such a great and comprehensive education.

5 months old and full of spunk

In summary: it is the humans' responsibility—your responsibility—to do, from the very first day forward, everything (and everything in good time) to help Mutz's body, mind, soul, personality, and behavior develop in the best possible way. The aim and the result of your effort must be a Berner who, upon reaching adulthood, will be a viable canine individual and, simultaneously, a perfect companion who is adequately skilled to live with you in your world. In both roles—as a dog and as a doggy companion—your Bernese must be visibly, tail-waggingly happy. Once Mutz has entered your life, nothing releases you from your responsibility. Remember: at the end of his first year, your Berner is what you have made of him.

Berners have a reputation as gentle giants. This image is well deserved, provided that they are treated as family members, thoroughly educated, and conscientiously socialized. A well-rounded Berner can be trusted to be a reliable babysitter, a valiant

protector, a trustworthy escort, a loyal companion, and a congenial confidant. In short, they are a genuine friend to children of all ages.

Chapter 6

Your Adult Berner

EVERYDAY LIFE

Life with an adult Bernese Mountain Dog is a natural continuation of the previous period, although appropriate adjustments must be made for this new stage of life. For example, Anni's nutrition may have to be modified. Whether she continues to be fed twice daily or is now served only one meal a day depends on her constitution and her and her humans' lifestyle. Since bloat is not uncommon in this breed, two smaller meals are better than one large one so her stomach is not overfilled.

The quantity of food is determined by Anni's physical exertion. A Berner who spends most of her days dozing on the terrace will require a lower calorie intake than one who frequently goes hiking or backpacking in the mountains or is regularly engaged in tracking. An only Berner, like Anni, will usually be less active than ones who share their life with canine cousins, so her nutritional needs are lower and her meals must be reduced accordingly. The fact that Berners are normally good eaters (some are, in fact, real gluttons) and metabolize their food efficiently should also be taken into consideration. The amount of food required by an adult Berner is frequently overestimated by their humans. More Berners are overfed than underfed. Too much weight is unhealthy. If you keep a close eye on your Berner, you will easily see when it is time to reduce her daily caloric intake, or you may wish to talk to your vet about a day of fasting. Once Anni's ideal weight in proportion to her stature has been determined, it should be checked regularly on the veterinarian's scale.

Regarding the composition of meals, the same basic principles apply as with the young Berner. The following daily meal plan may be considered a basic guide for an adult Bernese:

Breakfast: A slice of whole grain bread with butter and/or cheese

Dinner: Approx. one lb. of beef, either raw or cooked in just a little water (add enough of the broth to the meal to make it moist without being soupy)

Two cups of cereal (grain flakes), alternating with noodles or rice

One grated carrot or other vegetable

One tablespoon of thistle, linseed, or cod liver oil

Half a clove of crushed garlic

A dose of a vitamin-mineral-trace element preparation (given per the label directions)

Two raw egg yolks per week

A fresh calf bone is good for the adult Berner, too

As a bedtime treat, a piece of cheese, a cup of yogurt or kefir, or some fresh seasonal fruit are good choices for Anni. Gelatin from cooked calf knuckles (or, if this is too much work, powdered gelatin from the pharmacy) is a great supplement for the prevention or treatment of joint diseases.

Anni's appetite is considerably greater than her desire for physical exercise, a characteristic she shares with many only Berners. She can usually be found lying down, watching her surroundings, dozing, and/or sleeping for hours (calluses on the elbows may be a result). She will get up once in a while to go for a leisurely walk around the yard, take a few sniffs, and relieve herself. Without any outside stimulus she will not, however, move any farther—or faster—away from the house.

While, for obvious reasons, a large yard is great for Anni, it is not a substitute for regular and extensive walks. After all, it is no fun for a Berner to sniff only his or her own pee all the time. As a rule of thumb, a mature Bernese like Anni needs to be walked off-leash at least two hours every day, preferably for one hour in the morning and again in the late afternoon or early evening. On weekends, longer periods of activity should be a matter of course. Long walks are also important because Anni does not normally run and thus tire herself out as other breeds do. Instead, she normally accompanies her humans at a slow trot. Such long, leisurely walks are one of a Berner Senn's greatest pleasures. Having her nose to the ground, sniffing from smell to smell, is such a delight for Anni that she might almost forget the presence of her human companions. But only almost. Without them the walk would really be only half as enjoyable. Even if they don't join her in sniffing around, they are with her—and that's what counts. These regular strolls are Anni's absolute favorite pastime and the best part of her daily routine. She longs for them, full of expectation, even if she does not express this by impatiently nagging her folks. When the moment comes and you are about to fetch your comfy walking shoes, Anni will instantly be wide awake and full of excited anticipation, barking and bouncing and dancing around, unable to contain her joy. Nothing gives her greater pleasure than to go out with you. The only other time she shows such exuberance and bliss is when you return home from a trip without her—even if you have only been gone for five minutes.

Regarding sleep, essentially no changes need be made. An adult Berner, like an adolescent, can sleep like a log. Just look at Anni. Her gorgeous appearance is living proof of the effectiveness of beauty sleep. In Anni's daily life, every period of physical activity or mental strain is immediately compensated for by a good long nap. Periods of inactivity are spent slumbering. The less active her humans and the less going on in and around the house, the more she will sleep.

Body care

A Bernese Mountain Dog is an awesome sight, and Anni is no exception. Her striking appearance is mainly due to the natural beauty of her magnificent coat. Although largely dirt-resistant and self-cleaning (much like a good oriental rug), the coat does require regular combing and brushing (at least twice a week). The only tools needed for this are a coarse and a medium-spaced steel comb or rake, and two brushes—one with steel pins, the other with boar bristles. Matting should not occur on a well-cared for Berner; if, however, there are some dense mats, they have to be cut off. Combing and brushing must be particularly thorough during the seasonal change of coat (shedding). When grooming, one starts with the coarse side of the comb to separate the hair, especially behind the ears and at the trousers. Then use the medium side to comb the entire coat thoroughly. After that, brush the whole body with the steel brush, first against and then with the natural direction of the hair. Next, brush Anni with the bristle brush to bring out the natural sheen of her coat. A light rub down with a soft, moist cloth or chamois will add the finishing touch. A healthy Berner whose coat is regularly groomed this way, who gets well-balanced food, and who is given lots of outdoor exercise will always have a naturally beautiful, shining, pleasant-smelling coat.

Butchers are a Berner's best friend

Anni is bathed once or twice a year. Too-frequent bathing strips the skin of its natural oil barrier, which can lead to dehydration, skin irritation, and possibly an increased susceptibility to allergies. It also dries the hair, which removes Anni's natural protection against cold, wet, and dirt. Except for medical reasons (e.g., parasites, skin diseases) or when the coat is severely soiled (like after rolling in fresh manure), one or two baths a year (spring and fall) are sufficient. A special mild

Ready to don the traditional Berner collar

non-drying shampoo made just for dogs is best. Before a bath, comb loose hair out of the coat, protect Anni's ears with cotton balls, and cover her eyes with a cloth. The water should be lukewarm. Shampoo her carefully from tail to head, talking to her all the while. When working at Anni's head, keep her ear flaps closed with one hand. Don't forget to wash the spaces between the toes and the genital and anal areas. Rinse thoroughly, then rinse again. (Now you will be grateful for having taught puppy Anni to stand still!) When everything is done, allow Anni to run, shake herself, roll in the grass, and run some more. After that, rub her down with a towel and leave the rest to the sun and the air. Once Anni's coat is completely dry (which, admittedly, will take hours), brush it thoroughly. She will look gorgeous.

Other elements of routine body care include inspecting your Berner's entire body, regularly and carefully, for ticks during warm weather. Since the hair between the pads of the feet mats easily, which can cause Anni pain when walking (especially in winter when snow clumps between the toes and pads), it should be cut off with a pair of curved, blunt-ended shears. When doing this, the hair around the feet may also be clipped a little. Otherwise, no scissors will ever touch Anni's coat. Because she gets sufficient exercise, she will not normally need to have her toenails clipped. If it is necessary, use a special nail clipper, taking special care not to cut the quick. If in doubt, let your vet perform this procedure. Ordinary eye discharge (little gobs of whitish goo) can be wiped away with a tissue or a clean, soft, lint-free cloth. However, if you note a secretion of any other color from the eyes, report it to your vet. Check Anni's ears regularly, too. Loose hairs in the outer ear or at the entrance of the auditory canal, which can cause the dog to shake her head and scratch, can be carefully removed with a cotton swab—but never poke the swab into the ear. Wipe off ear wax with a cotton swab or soft cloth. A special cleansing solution will be prescribed if medically indicated (e.g., blockage of the ear canal, ear mites, otitis), but use such preparations only on a veterinarian's order.

Check Anni's teeth at least once a week. The formation of plaque and tartar varies from Berner to Berner. It is influenced by the composition of his or her saliva, age, food, water, and other factors. If plaque develops—even though Anni gets good chews such as pieces of stale bread crust or calf bones—her teeth ought to be cleaned regularly using a small toothbrush and a special doggy toothpaste. Brushing Anni's teeth will be easy if you gently familiarized her with the procedure when she was a puppy. Should tartar develop in spite of regular preventive dental hygiene, it is best removed by a veterinarian (usually under general anesthesia). Males must be checked for any yellowish discharge from the prepuce of the penis (balanoposthitis). If necessary, the penis and sheath are rinsed with an appropriate solution following your vet's advice. Observe female Berners for any unusual secretions from the vulva. Consult your veterinarian if you note anything abnormal. Needless to say, you must check the anal area regularly for cleanliness. Should feces stick to the anal hair, remove it gently with a soft cloth and warm water (if fresh) or an old comb (if dry).

A new dimension to life

In spite of its general seamlessness, life with a mature Bernese Mountain Dog will gradually take on a new dimension and quality. A Berner who in its first year was carefully educated will now be a reliable, predictable, cooperative, trouble-free, perfect partner for any situation life may bring.

Now the time, energy, care, and consistency you invested in Anni during her first months are really paying off. The more activities she and her human partner undertake together, the more closely they will bond. Now the time has come when dog and human truly live together. Their shared experience has a unique quality thanks to the special traits of the Bernese Mountain Dog.

Like every Berner, Anni is an affectionate, loving bear. She cannot get enough of the closeness, warmth, tenderness, and touch of her humans. She will claim her caresses in her own special way, if necessary. She will poke her humans with her nose; lay her chin on Mom's knee with unmistakable expectation in her eyes and on her face; nudge her nose, softly yet firmly, under a human arm; raise a paw to give a gentle tap; or sit on Dad's feet, snuggling against his legs, head thrown back, throat and chest offered for patting and stroking and scratching and rubbing and ruffling. A Berner's ways of demanding affection are miraculously manifold and exceptionally effective.

Regular brushing maintains that beautiful coat

A Bernese Mountain Dog is a highly sensitive soul. Regardless of what people may infer from Anni's massive body and imposing head, she is a friend of subtle sounds. She dislikes loud voices. One must speak to her as one would to a human being, now with child-like sweetness, later with grown-up earnestness. Anni wants to hear love and respect in the voices of her humans. Should there ever be a reason to reprimand her, there is no need for loud scolding. A tone of voice that is ever so slightly reproachful will suffice to motivate a Berner to seek peace with a wagging tail and eyes begging for forgiveness.

Berners have a great sense of humor. Anni can be a real goofball. She loves having fun with—and sometimes making fun of—her humans. She revels in hearing them laugh. She adores playing tug-of-war or hide-and-seek, being the first to catch the ball, trying to outrun her humans, wrestling on the ground, and frolicking in the powdery snow— anything, really, as long as it is a shared activity.

A Berner Senn is also a sucker for tranquility. The prime qualities that Anni values in her family's life are love, peace, and harmony. At the slightest hint of discord or a minor argument between her humans, Anni will wedge herself between them, seeking to restore peace. She will not hesitate to use all the facilities she can muster: an insistent nose poke or punch, a reproachful bark, a warning growl, or even impatiently grabbing the guilty party (and she can be trusted to know who started it) by the sleeve and pulling him or her away from the scene. And mercy on the human who would dare to raise a hand against the significant other! That would spell the end of Anni's tolerance.

A Bernese is charming and amiable even when jealous. When her humans embrace each other lovingly, Anni wants to be part of it. If she cannot manage to push her way between them, she may snatch the nearest object lying around—a shoe, a toy, a towel—and run off in an attempt to attract her folks' attention.

A Berner is adaptable to the point of self-sacrifice. There is no place too uncomfortable, no path too arduous, no climate too inclement, no strain too burdensome, if only Anni can be with her humans. To be excluded from the company of her family is the most severe punishment of all for her. Should that happen, her expression will very effectively communicate her feelings. The Bernese Mountain Dog is capable of displaying countless facial expressions: cheerful, annoyed, impatient, bored, reluctant, dreamy, philosophical, pensive, depressed, majestic, sulking, angry, unapproachable, inviting, attentive, warning, confused, haughty, devoted, disapproving, mischievous, maliciously gleeful, disgusted, indulgent, grateful, dignified, content, happy, proud. A Berner's countenance will display the range of his or her feelings, moods, and states of mind.

"Did I really **need** a bath?"

Active life

A Bernese Mountain Dog's life is always a reflection of his or her humans' lives. It can be quiet and contemplative, monotonous and boring, or eventful, varied, interesting, and exciting. Anni needs to be permitted to share a rich life with her humans, filled with activities suitable to her physique and nature, teeming with tasks that give her a sense of importance, and rich in joint undertakings that strengthen their bond.

Alter egos

One of the Berner's myriad facial expressions

Needless to say, Anni is allowed to participate in every aspect of normal family life. She will accompany her humans everywhere: shopping, visiting friends, taking the car to be serviced, picking up a guest from the train station, or taking part in an outing with the bowling club. Of course, it will also be a normal part of life that she will occasionally have to stay at home alone. Having been properly prepared as a puppy, she will tolerate being left alone for a few hours with perfect composure.

Like every Berner, Anni is quite content to lie in the grass with her humans, drowsing, dreaming, watching the clouds, enjoying the warmth of the ground, the fragrance of flowers, and the humming of bumblebees. As Berners are wont to do, she will listen for hours, with patience and appreciation, to stories her folks tell her. And she will watch them spend an afternoon working in the garden with attentive, untiring fascination.

With a Berner you can—depending on your preferences and physical condition—go walking, hiking, or jogging. When jogging, some common sense rules must be observed. This activity must be limited to the cooler times of the day and year. Upon leaving the house, Anni needs ample time to sniff around and relieve herself. Then you can begin to jog (preferably on a shady forest trail) at a leisurely speed with the dog off-leash beside you, always adjusting your pace to that of the dog. If Anni stops to sniff, you stop, too. Start again when she is ready to continue. A mature Berner who, like Anni, is in good shape and accustomed to jogging, will trot along happily and tirelessly for three or four miles (five or six km)—provided that she is allowed to make comfort stops at will and that it is really she who sets the pace. It goes without saying that longer activities and outings must be planned so that there are opportunities for the dog to have a drink on the way. If necessary, take along a supply of water. Anni, who has been acquainted with a backpack, is happy and proud to carry her own lunch box and water bottle.

When planning for activities during the spring and summer, the well-being of the dog must be given special consideration. A Berner can quickly overheat in warmer temperatures due to the thickness and darkness of his coat. In summer, therefore, Anni must be taken for her walks very early in the morning and late in the evening. During the heat of the day, she should rest in a shady, cool spot of her own choosing. Bernese prefer cooler and downright cold temperatures, and they worship the snow. Anyone who has ever watched a Berner rolling in a frost-covered meadow, catching snowflakes in the air, leaping and diving with his rump elevated as if genuflecting to the snow gods, romping and tunneling through powdery drifts, turning somersaults and skidding on his back, knows that winter is truly the Berner's favorite season. The joy of winter walks can be spoiled only by pain caused by clumps of snow caught between the toes and pads. This can be prevented to some extent by keeping the hair between the toes trimmed short and by applying petroleum jelly or udder balm on the pads before going out.

Apart from allowing Anni to be a full-fledged family companion, you can also share special activities with her. One can always rely on the breed's inherent desire to work. A Berner's enthusiasm for taking on tasks is tremendous. Thus, Anni is happy and content if she can accomplish something, anything, for and with her humans. Anyone who has had the opportunity to watch Bernese working as draft dogs on a Swiss dairy farm, their eager excitement while waiting to be harnessed to their cart, and their dexterity, power, agility, and pride in pulling the wagon laden with heavy milk churns, will realize that the physical abilities and the natural desires of these dogs are ideally suited to carting. Carting has become an increasingly popular activity among many Bernese fanciers around the world as well as an established element of club events. A Berner may also enjoy working towards a Companion Dog or Canine Good Citizen title, training and performing in Obedience, Tracking, Search and Rescue, Avalanche, or any other activity (provided their humans also enjoy it). Running an agility course is an activity the dogs may enjoy (although a typical Berner doesn't exactly seem to have been born for it) and that helps to keep them (and their humans) in good shape. Some Bernese are even known to be willing and talented partners for their humans in Freestyle Obedience or Dog Dancing. Another activity for which Bernese Mountain Dogs are naturally gifted is therapy work—in any form, with any kind of clientele having any kind of condition, and with people of any age.

A sound, mature Berner makes a great jogging partner (in moderation)

Going for a ride in the car is, of course, an established part of the life of a worldly Bernese like Anni. Having been accustomed to such travel as a puppy, she continues to love it. After all, every ride means more time spent doing things with and being close to her humans. It doesn't matter whether the vehicle is a van, a station wagon, or a subcompact—even the smallest car has enough room. Regardless of the size of the vehicle, the following items should always be on board: a container with fresh water, a small supply of food, a bowl, a blanket, a towel, a comb and brush, some cotton swabs, a little petroleum jelly or bag balm, a pair of tick tweezers, a few poop bags, a handful of treats, an extra collar and leash, and, during warmer weather, a spray bottle of cold water (best stored in a cooler) to help prevent overheating. At the slightest hint of a heat stroke (rapid, shallow breathing; rapid pulse; high body temperature; weakness; dizziness; nausea; collapse), a Berner must be taken to the nearest veterinarian immediately.

Content with his human

At regular intervals, Anni's people stop to let her stretch her legs and relieve herself. No dog's eyes should be exposed to forceful winds, which means that Anni should not be allowed to stick her head out the window while the car is moving. In the summer, only a vehicle with air conditioning should be used for rides with her. Anni must never, never be left alone in the car during warm weather, not for any length of time and not even with the windows rolled down and the sun roof open. A sufficiently large crate can be used to provide extra protection for Anni in case of an accident. One absolutely critical safety rule is this: when the door or hatch is opened, Anni must always remain seated until she is called out. Where there is traffic, she must be put on leash before jumping out.

Needless to say, Anni always accompanies her family on their holidays. However, a vacation shared with a Berner Sennenhund is subject to some restrictions. Forget about the cycling tour in Britanny, the cruise on the Nile, or the grand tour to the museums of Rome. Daytime surfing, disco nights? Not with a Berner. Travel to countries with quarantine regulations has to be ruled out. Exposing Anni to the stress and risk involved in flying? No way! And the climate at the holiday site must be tolerable for a thick-pelted dog, which means that if it has to be Spain, it definitely cannot be in the summer. Although staying at a hotel is not a problem for a Berner with good manners (in most parts of Europe, anyway), a holiday apartment or chalet, a mountain cabin, or a seaside cottage will obviously be better. The really important thing, though, is not only to take Anni along, but also to have her partake in all the holiday activities. A family trip across country in a motor home is heaven on earth for a Berner Sennenhund.

Consideration for others

If you wish to have your Berner accompany you almost everywhere, you will depend to a great extent on the understanding and tolerance of your fellow humans. The willingness of

Some Berners even enjoy agility

other people to accept a strange dog (and a large one, at that) as a member of society will be directly proportional to how positive an impression the dog makes on them. This requires that Anni be well educated in the proper behavior for life in human society (e.g., she does not jump around in the streetcar, does not sit drooling beside the restaurant table, does not poke her nose into strangers' crotches or behinds, does not bark at people in the street). Of course, it is not all up to the Berner; the dog's human partner must be considerate of the feelings of others. You must acknowledge and respect the fact that not everyone goes into raptures at the sight of a Bernese. Other people are certainly entitled not to share your love of dogs. It is also important that in the presence of other people, Anni is always kept on lead and at a close heel. At the sight of another person (with or without a dog) outdoors, Anni should be called back and leashed immediately. Only if the other person signals that they would be comfortable with your dog off-leash should you release the dog again. Before Anni is taken to town, on a walk through the neighborhood, to a friend's house, to the vet's, or anywhere else, be sure that she has relieved herself in an appropriate place. Still, keep a poop bag on hand in case of an accident. At the sight of small children, Anni is always closely heeled. To a three-year-old child, a Berner Sennenhund looks like a giant creature. If, however, the

parents consent, the child will be allowed to pat and hug the dog (who should be sitting or lying down). Of course, all of the above is nothing but Social Behavior 101, which is a matter of course for anyone who wants to be worthy of sharing his or her life with a Bernese Mountain Dog.

The evening of life

Those who have had the good fortune to share many years with a Bernese Mountain Dog do not need be told about the changes and the resulting adjustments that accompany old age. It is obvious that the older Berner must be treated with even more respect and consideration than before. Needless to say, she will be granted privileges that were formerly forbidden, from cleaning the occasional ice cream bowl to lying on the couch once in a while. Of course, you will tolerate with a smile the new foibles that Anni may develop in her senior years. It goes without saying that you will show the utmost consideration for her changing physical and psychological condition. You will take into account that her agility will diminish, her senses will weaken, her sensitivity will increase, your walks together will shorten in length but increase in number, that her sleep will be longer and deeper, and that both the amount and type of food she eats will have to be adjusted (she

A venerable veteran Berner

will need fewer calories, more vitamins and minerals, and food that is particularly easy to digest). For obvious reasons, you will be extra careful not to expose Anni to high temperatures or let her lie on cold, wet ground. And, naturally, visits to the veterinarian for checkups will become more frequent. As Anni's lifelong human partner you will know all this, of course. After all, life with an aging Berner is not a situation into which one is thrown without warning, but a state that has come about gradually with the passing of your shared years.

When you have enjoyed the joy and privilege of having had a Bernese by your side for, hopefully, ten years or more, you do not need to be told what it means to have to say the final farewell to your beloved friend. When you have fully shared a Berner's life, you will not leave him or her alone when the time comes to cross the Rainbow Bridge. Ideally, there will be a place near the house where your faithful companion can be laid to rest. The trusted family veterinarian will be glad to come and render the final service in the familiar surroundings of Anni's home. Love will provide the strength you need to hold your soulmate in your arms and look back into those soft, trustful, knowing eyes. In this last, long, loving mutual gaze lies the solace and the bliss that springs from the knowledge that everything has been given and everything has been received.

A Bernese Mountain Dog grows fast but matures slowly. It may well take three or four years for a Berner's body (and mind) to mature fully. This series illustrates the progress of a male Berner from puppy to senior.

▲ Newborn

Circle of Life

▲ 5 weeks

▼ 2 months

▲ 4 months

▼ 6 months

▲ 2 years

▼ 3 years

▲ 4 years

▼ 6 years

▲ 8 years

▼ 9 years

▲ 9 years, 2 months

World Champion/Best of Breed, female, World Show in Bern (The poster says "The world's most beautiful dogs have come to Bern!")

Chapter 7

Showing Bernese— European Style

SHOWS – TITLES – CLASSES – GRADES

Shows

Dog exhibitions are the showcase of canine breeding. At a show, breeders present the results of their "creative" efforts and submit them to a special form of quality control. Dog shows are also competitive events. Breeders and their dogs venture into competition with others; as a result, they learn where their dogs stand within the breed. The criterion for assessing the quality of a dog is always the breed Standard as interpreted by a licensed judge, before the eyes of an interested and, for the most part, knowledgeable audience.

For breeders, a show is also a marketplace for information. Here they can see other dogs, sharpen their eyes for the merits and faults of their own dogs and those of others, discover potential partners for their bitches, and have an excellent opportunity to exchange views and experiences with other breeders. Aside from that, dog shows also fulfill a social function: one sees and is seen; chats a little here and gossips a bit there; criticizes the judges, or maybe rails about club officers; and one is—depending on the outcome—proud of oneself and one's dog or envious of the others. If nothing else, a dog show is an interesting event.

The sum of the individual achievements at a dog show offers insight into the overall state of the breed regarding conformation, soundness, and temperament. In that respect, a show also serves as an important source of information for the respective club, because it reveals to what extent the club's breeding concepts, strategies, and control mechanisms have been effective. At the same time, a show is an instrument through which the club can steer the direction of breeding—for good or bad. At a dog show in German-speaking Europe, a club, through its judges can set signals and throw switches; can encourage positive trends and curb negative ones; can determine the success or the failure of a certain line of breeding; and can place one dog in the limelight and another in the shade. All of this is perfectly acceptable as long as it happens in the best interest of the breed and convincingly aims to maintain or improve the breed.

A dog show is not only for clubs and breeders. It is also an opportunity for regular Berner people to get an expert judge's opinion on their darling (it goes without saying that, for them, Anni

or Mika will always and forever be the most beautiful Berner in the world). For many, their first appearance at a show will be their last, regardless of what the judge may say—perhaps they only went as a favor to the breeder of their dog. Others, however, may catch the bug; their ambition will be aroused, and they go a second and a third time, until—before they know it—they are hooked on showing. Last month, they and their Berner made the first cut; this week fourth place; and next time, perhaps, the blue ribbon (which, in Europe, is red). And if not next time, then it will happen the time after, for sure.

The following description of the German dog show system basically applies in all FCI member countries. There are two kinds of exhibitions. First, there are specialty breed shows that are conducted by a breed club. At such a show, which can be regional or national, dogs compete for a national championship challenge certificate (*Certificat d'Aptitude au Championat*, CAC). Given the short distances in Europe, even a regional specialty show draws entries not only from Germany, but also from neighboring countries such as Switzerland, Denmark, and the Netherlands, to name but a few. Second, there are international all-breed shows held by the German kennel club or *Verband für das Deutsche Hundewesen* (VDH), where, in addition to the CAC, there is also a CACIB to be earned (*Certificat d'Aptitude au Championat International de Beauté*), the challenge certificate for the title International Champion. These all-breed shows are a collection of specialty shows under one roof and under the umbrella of the VDH. The mechanics of the show—ring organization, judging assignments, trophies, etc.—is delegated to a breed club. If more than one club for a single breed is recognized, as is the case for Berners in Germany (the DCBS and SSV), the kennel club apportions the shows to each club based on the size of their membership and the number of dogs registered with that club. A larger club will be allocated a greater number of shows than a smaller club. CAC shows are held outdoors or indoors; CACIB shows are usually held indoors. The latter are benched shows, meaning that wire crates or open wooden boxes are provided, which the dogs are expected to occupy when not in the ring. Dogs that do not hold a pedigree recognized by the FCI are excluded from any of these events. In other words, a Bernese Mountain Dog will only be admitted if he or she has a pedigree recognized by either the German DCBS or SSV, the Swiss KBS, the Austrian VSSÖ, or, if from another country, a pedigree issued and recognized by that country's national kennel organization. A club member may not participate in any event (show or other) conducted by a canine organization, registry, or Berner club that is not recognized by the kennel club. Likewise, membership in or breeding activity involving a breeder and dog from such an organization is not tolerated by the kennel club system. Judging in all the FCI member countries is uniformly based on the FCI breed Standard as developed by the breed club(s) of a breed's country of origin. Thus, Berners are always judged against the same Standard whether at a show in France or Finland, Israel or Italy, Monaco or Mexico, Peru or Portugal, Sweden or Switzerland. Only when it comes to placing the first four dogs in a class (see below) are the dogs compared with the competition.

It bears repeating that breed specialist judges are trained, examined, and certified by the breed club (and then recognized by the kennel club). The number of such Bernese specialist judges is small: in Germany, they number about a dozen; in Switzerland, hardly ten.

Titles

At dog shows, challenge certificates for the following titles are up for competition (separately for dogs and bitches):

German Champion (*Dt.Ch.*; awarded by the VDH). Requirements: four CACs issued by the VDH. A challenge certificate is awarded at the discretion of the judge to the winners of the open class (dogs and bitches) and the champion class (dogs and bitches). The four CACs must be earned under three different judges. In other words, even a number of, say, nine CACs from a total of two judges would not earn a dog a championship.

German Champion (*Dt.Ch.*; awarded by a Club, such as the DCBS or SSV). Requirements are as above except that only one CAC per sex is awarded, i.e., the overall best dog and the overall best bitch at the show. Certificates are issued by the respective club (each club may award its own German championship). The CAC can only be awarded—at the discretion of the judge—if the dog has previously won the Open Class or the Champion Class with the grade Excellent (V, see below).

International Champion (FCI). Requires four CACIBs; this certificate is issued by the FCI. Again, the CACIB is awarded at the discretion of the judge only to the winning dog and bitch. The four CACIBs must be earned under three different judges in three different countries.

A requirement that applies to all three championships is that a period of one year and one day must elapse between the first and the fourth challenge certificate earned. Thus, even if Mika won, say, seven CACs and/or CACIBs in the course of one summer (which is virtually impossible due to the small number of shows and the strong competition), only the first three would count toward his National or International Championship. He would not receive the title unless he earned another CAC or CACIB at least one year after the first one. The objective of this requirement is to ensure that only a dog who proves to be of top quality over a considerable period of time can become a champion. Even if there were show clusters and show circuits (which there are not), there would be no "cluster champions" and no "circuit champions." The minimum age for obtaining any of the challenge certificates is 15 months, meaning that a certificate cannot be won from the puppy or junior class. The award represents one leg toward the championship, which implies that the dog is worthy of that title. The Champion, by definition, can only be a fully mature dog of outstanding quality that comes very close to being an ideal specimen as described by the Standard. Champions, after all, are the models for the breed. A Berner, who is a slow-maturing dog anyway, will rarely be able to earn a CAC or CACIB before 2½ or 3 years of age.

Another obstacle on the road to a Championship is the large number of dogs and the small number of shows. In Germany, hardly more than a dozen all-breed shows are held each year, with less than twenty Berner club specialties under the SSV and half a dozen under the DCBS. In Switzerland, only two or three CACIB/CAC shows are held annually, and only one national club specialty every other year. In Austria, the number of shows is equally small. Thus, to use an extreme example, a Swiss Bernese has only two or three chances a year to win a CAC or CACIB in his or her home country. Conversely, the Berner population is fairly large and the distances are short. As a result, the number of entries at these shows is quite large. It is not uncommon to see 20 or 30 males and usually even more bitches in the Open Class. These dogs range in ages from 1½ to 6 or 7 years (the Veteran Class starts at age 8). Needless to say, it is extremely difficult for a young dog to stand its ground against all the fully matured entries. Plus, it is extremely difficult for an Open Class winner to defeat the winner of the Champion Class for Best of Sex and, hence, for the CAC and/or CACIB. Thus, it is quite an ordeal to earn a National or an International Championship, and it is well nigh impossible for a Berner to finish the Championship before it is 4 or 5 years old, if ever. Therefore,

Winning at a show in Switzerland (especially Bern) is always something special

Traditional Swiss folk costume in the show ring adds a special touch of authenticity

the number of Champions is extremely small. At no time are there more than four or five titleholders in Germany, and two or three in Switzerland. That explains why, even at big events, very few, if any, Champions are entered.

In Switzerland, the title Swiss Champion (*Schweizer Schönheitssieger*) is conferred if a dog has won three CACs under two different judges. In view of the tough competition (which always includes dogs from other countries) and given that there are only two or three shows per year, it is easy to understand why it is next to impossible for a dog to earn a Swiss Championship. In fact, there are usually even fewer Swiss Champions than International Champions in Switzerland. Although the International Champion title carries the most prestige, there can be no doubt that the Swiss Championship is the most difficult to earn and hence is the most valuable of all titles for a Berner. A foreign Berner's win or placement at a show in Switzerland is always a very special achievement.

In addition to these Championship titles, there are also several "one-day" titles. These are mentioned here because such titles may be found on the pedigrees of European Berners. Each year, the German VDH holds two special all-breed shows. At one, the title *Bundessieger* (Federal Winner), and at the other, the title *Europasieger* (European Winner) is awarded to both the best dog and the best bitch. The annual FCI World Show, which offers the title World Champion, is held in a different member country each year. The value of any of these one-day titles obviously depends largely on the competition present on that day. The title World Champion won in a distant country with an entry of, say, three Bernese, is obviously not quite the same—though formally of equal value—as the same title received at the World Show in Bern, Switzerland.

Two further events must be mentioned here. The national specialty show of a Bernese breed club (which in Germany is held only at three-year intervals) is usually an impressive showcase of the breed, and the title Best of Specialty Show (*Clubsieger*)—even though it does not qualify for entry in the Champion Class—is highly coveted and greatly esteemed. The same is true in Switzerland, where the KBS holds a national specialty show every two years. During the alternate years, the club conducts a specialty show for male Berners only (*Rüdenschau*). Such a show emphasizes the traditionally dominant role and reputation of the male animal in breeding. It is—more than any other show—a marriage market for Berners and a public relations event for active stud dogs whose owners wish to present them to a larger audience, in order to maintain or expand their market position. Many young, up-and-coming dogs are also shown with the hope that they will be "discovered"—that they will attract the attention of breeders who are looking for a suitable mate for their bitch.

Classes

The Puppy Class (*Jüngstenklasse*, JüK) is for Berners between 6 and 9 months of age. Since a puppy is not yet sufficiently developed to be judged the same way as a mature dog, it will only get a general rating like "very promising" (*vielversprechend*, vv), "promising" (*versprechend*, vsp) or "little promising" (*wenig versprechend*, wv). People do not show their puppies primarily because they want them judged according to the Standard, but because they enjoy their little family addition and are proud to present him or her at such an event. They also want to familiarize their puppy with the atmosphere, noise, crowds, the presence of other dogs, and the procedure in the show ring while ensuring that the little one has a positive experience at the event.

The Junior Class (*Jugendklasse*, JK) is for dogs from 9 to 18 months of age; and a dog over 15 months may, and a dog over 18 months must, be entered in the Open Class (*Offene Klasse*, OK). The Open Class always has the largest number of entries, and it also is the class with the widest age bracket (from 1½ to 7 years), with young and middle-aged dogs forming the majority. Many bitch owners stop showing their dog once she has successfully attended the two shows required for the breed assessment; other people stop if their dog does not do well, since there is no way that such a dog could be "finished," meaning that he would get his championship eventually if shown often enough.

Only very few dogs are ever entered in the Champion Class (*Championklasse*, CHK). This is not surprising, given what has been said above about gaining a Championship. Champions are the rare

top specimens of the breed. It is not unusual to find no dogs entered in this class at all. Even at large shows, the number of Champions present can be counted on the fingers of one hand.

The Honorary Class (*Ehrenklasse*) is reserved exclusively for dogs who have already earned the title of International Champion. Since these dogs have already made it into the Berner Hall of Fame, they do not compete for any award or title except Best of Breed (which does not count towards anything, but is the icing on the cake).

Dogs over 8 years of age are shown in the non-competitive Veteran Class (*Veteranenklasse*, VK). Participation in this class is usually very small, a fact that is regrettable and difficult to understand. After all, breeders who can present dogs that are older, healthy, vital, and perhaps even of beautiful conformation have surely reached the ideal goal of any responsible breeding program and deserve the highest recognition. Breed clubs should do everything to promote the showing of veteran dogs. Breeders and owners of older Berners should be encouraged to present their dogs, and they should be commended and rewarded for doing so. The Veteran Class deserves to be given maximum attention. A Parade of Veterans, such as that held at the National Specialty of the Bernese Mountain Dog Club of America, is an awesome sight to behold and should be the absolute highlight of any Berner show.

Three other events deserve special mention here: the presentation of Kennel Groups (*Zuchtgruppen*), Progeny Groups (*Nachzuchtgruppen*), and Brace Class (*Paarklasse*). A Kennel Group consists of at least three dogs bred by one breeder. A Progeny Group consists of a parent and a minimum of five offspring from at least two different litters. A Brace consists of a male and a female dog owned by one exhibitor. Any dog entered in one of these classes must have been rated at least Good (*Gut*) in a regular class. These groups are assessed with particular attention to uniformity of type and soundness—that is, phenotypical family likeness. The significance and value of these events is obvious. After all, consistent quality over generations is a better indicator of successful breeding than a single dog's class win or championship.

Grades

At an exhibition, a dog will receive one of the following grades: Excellent (*Vorzüglich*, V); Very Good (*Sehr gut,* SG), Good (*Gut,* G), Adequate (*Genügend,* Ggd), or Disqualified (*Disqualifiziert,* Disq.). In Germany, an Excellent grade cannot be conferred in the Junior Class. The rationale is that a juvenile dog (younger than 15 months), by definition, cannot yet have reached excellence in conformation. A dog who will not stand for examination—for example, will not have his teeth or testicles checked—is excused from the ring without being graded. The four best dogs of each class are ranked. Typically, the ranking will be V1, V2, V3, and V4. If, however, the judge gave a V to only two dogs, then he will include the best two SG-graded dogs in the ranking. In that case, the ranking will be as follows: V1, V2, SG3, and SG4. The judge must write (or rather dictate to a ring secretary) a detailed critique on every dog. A copy of this evaluation stays with the club; the exhibitor also receives a copy. The grade is also entered on the pedigree, which must be submitted at the beginning of the show and will be returned only at the end of the show day. Interested individuals can obtain the judges' critiques by subscription from the respective club.

The critiques are characterized by general "doggy" language and the terminology of the breed Standard. Of course, a critique also reflects the personal rhetoric and eloquence of a judge. The following two critiques of the dog pictured on p. 40 are typical examples (this author's translation):

Judge A (Switzerland): "3.5 year old male, of medium size, with friendly head; dark eye, good ear carriage. Good back and croup, good tail carriage, bone structure commensurate with the dog's type; good stance and angulations, good colors, very beautiful coat. Scissors bite. Flowing movement. Grade: Excellent, V1."

Judge B (Germany): "3.5 year old, fully mature male; ideal coat and markings, a lot of type and charisma, very impressive head. Correct stance; front angulation excellent, rear angulation good. Balanced movement, with the rear treading just very slightly short because of the slightly less than ideal angle. Outstanding, balanced temperament. Excellent relationship with handler. Grade: Excellent, V1."

When judging in all classes is finished (usually by midafternoon), the first-placed dog from the Open Class and the winner of the Champion Class will compete against each other for the challenge certificate (CAC and/or CACIB). The award winner and the first-placed dog from the Junior Class will compete for Best Dog. The same procedure determines Best Bitch. Best Dog and

Dignity and modesty in victory
(World Champion, male,
World Show in Bern)

Best Bitch will then compete with the first-ranked dog and/or bitch from the Honorary Class or Classes for Best of Breed (BOB).

At international all-breed shows, the Best of Breed from each breed of a group (i.e., Bernese in FCI-Group 2, together with the short coated Swiss Sennenhunde and all the Watch, Guard, and Working Dogs), will compete for group winner. If the show is a two-day event, the group winners of each day will compete for Best of Day. At the end of the show, all Group Winners compete for Best in Show (BIS).

Show day

Once you have decided to show your handsome Berner boy, Mika, you should plan and prepare thoroughly. First, it is a good idea to attend a show without your dog. This will allow you to make yourself familiar with the protocol and the atmosphere characteristic of such an event. You will also learn what equipment is necessary or useful to take along (from a water bowl to a folding chair).

It is essential to have the dog in excellent physical condition and to present him in such a way that you bring out the best in him. Although every Bernese Mountain Dog is beautiful by nature, Mika's beauty will be enhanced if he is in perfect health, is well-nourished, exhibits an immaculate appearance, and displays impeccable behavior. All of these qualities combined will give onlookers an overall superb impression of your Berner. Also, each aspect must be considered over the long term. This is particularly important regarding ring behavior, which is best taught at puppy age. This is not to say that the puppy should explicitly be trained to become a show robot, but rather that the behavior required in the show ring is practically the same that is expected of any well-educated, well-mannered dog. In other words, a Berner Sennenhund who is shown need only to be able to stand, sit, walk, gait, and perform a correct U-turn—all at heel. The only difficulty is that all of these maneuvers must be performed in the presence of other dogs and in a very crowded space. The dog should be unimpressed by the hectic atmosphere, noise, and crowds of people. Also, he has to tolerate a thorough hands-on examination by the judge: head, muzzle, teeth, ears, neck, back, tail, chest, belly, legs, feet, and testicles. It is important that Mika stand reliably during this examination. His ability to stand still is all the more important because—unlike some other breeds—a Berner Sennenhund is not stacked in the show ring. Rather, he poses on his own on a loose leash, meaning that he naturally places himself in the most comfortable and hence the most advantageous (and the most revealing) stance. At a signal (verbal or visual) from you, Mika should stand like a statue—fully concentrated yet totally at ease, with an animated expression, slightly raised head, alert ears, and attentive eyes; with a straight front, rear legs parallel, one set slightly behind the other, and his tail hanging relaxed. He does it well and he enjoys doing it. After all, this is what he has practiced with you often enough at a fun match of a regional breed club, at a practice session at the local obedience school, on the market square, in a parking lot, and, of course, in the field behind the house.

Another important point is movement, which in the ring means a trot. At a dog show, Mika should demonstrate that he has a balanced, striding gait. This requires three things: first, Mika should have had ample opportunity to develop a good gait by trotting regularly, preferably on natural ground; second, he must have learned to trot on your left side on a loose leash; and third, that you yourself must be in good enough physical shape to be able to run easily around a show ring for five or ten minutes. After the judge has examined every dog (five to ten minutes each), he will move all the V-dogs around the ring again and again until he has made his selection. This is an activity that is definitely not for overweight Berners. It is important that you always watch Mika from the corner of your eye and adjust your speed so that he can move at his best. For you this means not too fast and not too slow, with steps neither too long nor too short. A dog on a leash can only move as well as his handler allows him. All of this works best only if a close and trusting relationship exists between you and Mika, if you have learned to make him understand what you expect of him and he has learned that it is fun to do things with you, and you have had shared experiences and mastered situations together in the past. If that is not the case, showing will be a torture that you should spare your Berner (and yourself).

Since Mika is regularly groomed, he does not need extensive beautification for a show; a thorough brushing is normally sufficient. If, however, a bath should be necessary (due to a particularly rustic life style), do not wait until the very last day before the show. Freshly-washed Berner hair does not lie naturally on the body because it has been deprived of its natural oil and therefore lacks its natural weight. Instead, it tends to stand up or be extra wavy (or even curly), especially on the rump. Professional grooming is unknown with European Berners. No grooming tables are used as all grooming is done at home, except for a final brushing. The only extra measure needed may be to trim the hair on the edge of the feet a little. The coat of a Bernese Mountain Dog is beautiful by nature and does not require cosmetic manipulation. A Berner is not puffed or fluffed, chalked or sprayed, scissored or sculptured. If nothing else, such preparations would be in violation of the kennel club show rules and would be penalized by the judge.

Best Veteran (10) and…

Berner shows in German-speaking Europe are, traditionally, a casual affair. There is comparatively little professionalism and showmanship; a bit more of both would be welcome at times. It is no surprise that overseas visitors have found the procedure in the show ring and the appearance of some Berners (and their handlers) at these shows a bit, well, rustic.

At a benched show, Mika is expected to spend most of the day in his wire crate or frontless wooden cubicle (the latter is equipped with a metal ring to which the leash can be fastened). It goes without saying that one of his humans always stays as close to Mika as possible. Now is the time that he needs his family the most (shows are truly family affairs). The situation is, after all, extremely stressful for the dog: the atmosphere is hectic; other dogs are left, right, behind, and in front; there is incessant barking (not from Berners, of course) and the constant babbling of strange voices; a thousand feet shuffling by; and a thousand strange smells (from French fries to French mustard to French perfume to French cigarettes). And all of this is happening at a time when Mika needs nothing else so much as quiet and calm. You must never forget that this is his day. His performance is what is important and, therefore, his well being has absolute priority. Today, more than ever, he is entitled to your complete attention.

As a matter of fairness, of course, you will congratulate the handlers of the first-placed dogs. These handlers, incidentally, will normally be the dogs' owners. Berner people (unless they are physically disabled) always show their own dogs. There are no professional handlers in German-speaking Europe, and certainly not with Berners. Regardless of the grade Mika received, let him feel that he did well— after all, he is and always will be the best and the most beautiful Berner in the world. The rest of the long day your Berner will spend, exhausted, in his crate or cubicle with you by his side. The rules of benched shows require that exhibitors stay until the end. After all, this is not only a contest for exhibitors and their dogs but also an informative event for an admission-paying audience that has a right to see the dogs until closing time. This also provides an excellent opportunity for the audience to get a firsthand impression of Berners, to pet them, ask questions, and get to know breeders. When at last it is time to drive home, for many it will have been the last dog show of their life (or of their dog's life); maybe because they received a disappointing critique of their dog, or

...Open Class Winner at a Swiss all-male specialty show

because they did not like the whole affair very much. For others, this day may mark the beginning of a new passion. If this enthusiasm is gratified simply for its own sake—if Mika is only seen, used, and abused as a tool to satisfy his human's ambition—then the sport is deprived of its ethical legitimacy. If, however, you and your Bernese are partners and you both share the pleasure and the joy of being together and doing things as a team, then, whether you win or not, dog shows can be fun for both of you.

Morning To Night

Chapter 8

Breeding
Your Berner

THE FEMALE SIDE OF THE COIN

Readers who expect to find a crash course on breeding Bernese
in the following pages will be disappointed. The inclusion of
chapters on breeding and raising puppies might easily be
misinterpreted as a suggestion that it is easy to breed dogs and
that it is normal to entertain the idea of breeding your own dog.
Far from it. To breed dogs means to co-create animate beings.

This is not a trivial task. In fact, it is too serious, too demanding, and fraught with too much
responsibility to be adequately dealt with in a short "how to" chapter, as if it were a recipe or an
instruction manual. Just as everyone is not meant to be a Berner person, not every Berner person is
meant to breed his or her dog.

The responsible breeding of dogs requires much more knowledge than just being aware of the
days when Britta can conceive, mating behavior, the duration of a pregnancy, how to build a
whelping box, canine obstetrics, and the nutritional needs of puppies. Anyone who is bold enough
to venture into co-creating animate beings should, first of all, examine his or her motives very
thoroughly and very critically. The following reasons never constitute legitimate justifications for
bringing even one Berner puppy into this world:

- Britta should have a litter at least once in her life, because it (allegedly) benefits her health
  and/or her psyche, or because it (supposedly) has a positive influence on her behavior, or
  because it is (as claimed by some) a remedy against false pregnancies, or because the
  experience of motherhood will be wonderful for her (or so you think);
- Witnessing the birth and the rearing of puppies is a wonderful, enriching, rewarding,
  educational experience for humans, and especially for their children;

The breeder bears responsibility for the well-being of the puppy—and the welfare of the entire breed

- The (supposed) profit from selling a litter of puppies will buy new kitchen appliances or will make a down payment for a new car.

This is not to say that no one should begin to breed Berners. After all, every breeder had to start sometime, and everyone who is blessed with a Berner companion owes his or her good fortune to a breeder. Without the courage to begin something new there can be no success. Breeding Berners can doubtlessly be an experience that will, in a variety of ways, bring satisfaction, joy, and happiness not only to the breeder but also to those who receive a puppy. In the end, everyone must decide for himself. However, it is essential that you very carefully and very seriously consider whether you are willing and able to meet all the demands which in the past you made—or should have made—on the breeder of your own Bernese.

It bears restating that breeding is more than just mating two dogs. A breeder must have a deep respect for animal life, a high sense of responsibility for the breed as whole and for each individual dog, a profound knowledge of canine obstetrics, and expert practical skills. It is not enough to have a breedable bitch and kennel facilities, even if that bitch possesses outstanding soundness, health, and conformation, and even if the kennel is heated, air conditioned, well lit, and surrounded by lush, green meadows. As a prospective breeder you must first closely study all aspects of the breed, know the breed's history, understand the breed's physical features and character traits, and internalize the breed Standard. You must also be aware of the health problems that afflict the breed. You must have insight into general biological matters and an understanding of complex genetic concepts. You must have a clearly defined breeding goal, and you must have the expertise necessary to accomplish this goal. Breeding requires both the theoretical knowledge of the diverse demands associated with raising puppies and the hands-on skills to effectively apply this knowledge in practice. Additionally, do you have and are you willing to commit the time and money necessary to breed dogs and raise puppies? Are you prepared to bear the health risks involved for Britta in pregnancy and birth (if there should be a birth)? Will you be strong enough to cope with the loss of one (or even all) of the precious puppies? Will you be able to bear the responsibility of "producing" puppies that may have deformities or health problems? Will you be strong enough to handle the emotional stress caused by the puppies' departure? Will you be able to find, assess, select, and—if need be—reject prospective buyers? Do you have the doggy know-how and the communication skills to guide your buyers to that perfect puppy and to instruct them about every possible question or problem they may have? Do you have the intention, the determination, and the means to test progeny efficiently? Are you prepared to keep track of all "your" puppies—not only from the first, but from every litter— throughout their lifetimes? Do you have the will and means to take on lifelong responsibility for the well-being of every single puppy? What if one of the puppies whom you have raised with love, care, and competence is later physically or temperamentally crippled through improper care, inadequate training, or even abuse by its new owners? What if one of your precious babies ends up with a backyard breeder or in a puppy mill? Will you be prepared and able to take back any of your dogs at any time, if necessary? Will you be willing and able to enforce the buy-back clause in your sales contract? Are you aware that there may be buyers who will not hesitate to take legal action should the puppy develop a specific health problem? These are just a few of the questions you must ask

yourself—and answer honestly. Breeding dogs can be a blissful but also a painful experience; it can reward, but it can also punish. As a breeder you must be prepared to accept not only the good, but also the bad and the ugly that inevitably accompanies breeding.

As a prospective breeder you should—in your own interest and in that of the breed—bear all this in mind when critically assessing your motives. Then you should undertake a realistic cost-benefit analysis. The costs should include any conceivable efforts, services, and risks; the benefits should include all the anticipated (but by no means guaranteed) satisfactions, joys, and feelings of success you will derive from the venture. If you are still determined to bring a litter of Bernese into this world after all this soul-searching, then may the best of luck and success be with you.

The male side of the coin

Much of what has been said about the female side of breeding also applies to the male. Anyone who intends to breed their male Berner with a Berneress will also engage in breeding and will, therefore, have to accept responsibility for his or her actions. There is one major difference, however. Whether or not Britta becomes a brood bitch depends solely on the decision of her humans (provided she has received her health clearances and has passed the breed assessment); whether Brix becomes a stud depends not only on his humans but on a number of factors that are beyond their control.

But first, why should anyone wish to offer their Berner companion as a stud? Of course, most stud owners have nothing but the improvement of the breed in mind. For some it is a well-meant, though perhaps naïve, attempt to provide their Berner buddy with sexual satisfaction. For others it may be the anticipated delight at recognizing the beauty, the sweet temperament, and the facial expression of their furry friend in his offspring. One person may take pride in the productive contribution of their four-legged partner to the breed; another may bask in the social recognition within the breed club that usually accrues to the owner of a popular stud dog. Whatever the reason, the person's ego will doubtlessly be flattered by the status of their successful stud. An additional incentive may be the prospect of financial reward for the dog's service ("a fast buck for a quickie"). However, things are not always as fast or easy or positive as one might think.

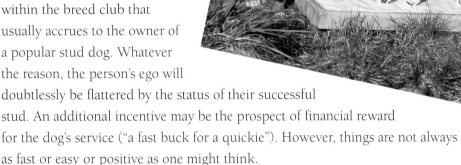

A breeder bears lifelong responsibility for each and every puppy

The road to success can be quite bumpy. It often resembles an obstacle course more than a highway. It is not enough to have a sound, typey, nicely-tempered Berner with the right bloodlines, all the necessary health clearances, and an excellent breeding certificate. Unless Brix is openly endorsed by the club's breed warden(s), he will first have to be successfully marketed. That means plenty of exposure at dog shows, taking out ads in canine magazines or club newsletters, having glossy business cards printed that show a flattering picture of your potential stud, and/or a home page on the Internet. It is a time-consuming, costly enterprise.

Once the prospective canine cha-cha boy has made his entrance upon the stage, everyone's attention will be drawn to him. What are his apparent virtues, and what are his flaws? How fast, how often, and by whom will he be used? What will he "produce"? Incidentally, not everyone will welcome the new torero. Suspicion, envy, badmouthing, and backstabbing may also be part of the game.

Stud dogs may—seasonally—get a lot of company, yet they tend to be lonely heroes. Most are protected, sheltered, and separated from the ordinary dog world. Studs are a rare sight on doggy playgrounds or at Berner outings for fear that they will sprain a limb or contract an infection. They live a mostly reclusive life—they are either on duty, preparing for it, or resting from it. Stud owners, too, are always under pressure. Their dog is expected to perform successfully with any bitch at any time. And if, for whatever reason, a mating cannot be accomplished—because it is too early, or too late, or Britta is not willing, or because Brix, from lack of interest or low libido or perhaps trusting his own instincts better than human plans, refuses to perform—in almost every case the blame will accrue to him alone. If a mating does not take, he is likely to be held responsible. And even if (and luckily this is the normal case) the breeding takes, Brix (or, rather, his human) is well advised not to rejoice too soon. It is best to wait to see what turns up in the whelping box. Only three pups? Poor sperm quality, for sure. Several stillborn pups? Probably a mating infection transmitted by the stud. If the offspring does not fully meet the breeder's expectations, he or she may easily forget that a puppy has two parents—it must be the father's fault! No matter what aspect of the pups is criticized—size, markings, rear angulation, eye color or ear set, tail carriage or coat texture, teeth or testicles—the stud is to blame! And if, two years later, one of the offspring shows any temperamental flaw, many will not bother to ask by whom and how the dog was educated, but rather "Who sired that dog?" The prospective owner of a stud dog must be aware that he or she needs to have a thick skin.

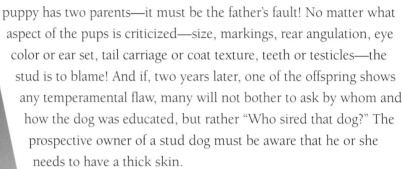

Admittedly, if everything goes well, the income from stud service is easy money—easier than the revenue gained from the sale of puppies, anyway. Stud fees, however, do not come without risk to Brix. If you consider offering your Bernese at stud, you should be aware of the hazards involved. All stud dogs are used; some are abused; others are used up. The stories are legion: bite wounds, infections, sprained limbs, circulatory failure, heart attack, and other hazards. A frequently used stud is under strain, both physically and emotionally. As soon as the car carrying Britta turns into the driveway, Brix will roar in excited, anxious anticipation. Days after she has left, he will continue to sniff out her scent marks with longing despair. Stud dogs suffer miserably if—despite all their amorous efforts—a visiting bitch will not permit them to perform their duty (that is, fulfill their desire). Some stud dogs may undergo a change in personality, become less affectionate towards their humans, or even become aggressive toward other males. The hopeful would-be owner of a Berner stud should bear all this in mind.

A stud and his human must be prepared to weather stiff winds

Incidentally, in German-speaking Bernerdom, studs render their services on home ground only. Brix would never be "loaned out" (sent away from his human family), just as Britta—regardless of the distance involved—would never be shipped to the stud unaccompanied by one of her folks. As mentioned earlier, artificial insemination is not considered an option.

To return to the issue of responsibility: as a prospective Berner stud owner you need to know more than just the technical procedure of mating dogs. You must, just as the owner of the bitch, possess detailed knowledge of the breed, genetic matters, anatomical facts, physiological processes, and hormonal conditions. You must, just like the breeder, follow ethical principles and accept responsibility for your part in the breeding of the individual litter, as well as that litter's role in the breed. If you do not want yourself and your dog to be used by others, you too must have a goal. This goal must be the same as that of the breeder: to co-create the best possible puppies in order to maintain or improve the quality and well-being of the breed. You, too, must do everything in your power to come as close as possible to this goal, and you must not do anything that is opposed to it.

There are more than a few people who believe that breeders alone determine the partners of a canine breeding, and hence they alone are responsible for the outcome and its significance for the breed. Such thinking reduces the stud owner's role to that of a procurer who is expected only to make the dog available to any bitch. As a stud owner, you have not only the right but also the obligation to assess the compatibility and appropriateness of each and every breeding. You are morally required to cast more than a superficial glance at the bitch's pedigree and breeding certificate; you must carefully analyze her ancestry, conformation, temperament, health clearances, and breeding scores, and check their compatibility with the respective features of your own dog. This will not only benefit the breed, but will also be in your own best interest as any negative breeding outcome will reflect badly on your dog and decrease his value. If you are in doubt, decline participation in the prospective breeding. Of course, your responsibility also includes—with or without the support of "your" breeder(s)—keeping abreast of the development and fate of the puppies sired by your stud (and providing help when the breeder is unwilling or unable to help) for the sake of the individual dog, in the interest of the breed, and for the benefit of your own conscience.

A stud dog's life can be surprisingly lonely

In summary: If you dream of your Berner boy becoming a famous stud, you are well advised to evaluate your motives critically and to conduct the same cost-benefit analysis described above for the prospective breeder. Then, if you should decide to pursue your dream, may the best of luck and success be with you.

Berner Beauty

Chapter 9

Your Berner's Health

Berner Kira's state of health—like that of her humans—is largely
influenced by her lifestyle. Most diseases are not genetically
determined but are rather the result of disadvantageous living
conditions: inappropriate care, inadequate hygiene, malnutrition,
a polluted environment leading to the absorption of noxious
substances, physical over- or under-exertion, etc.
The best preventive health care, therefore, is always a
breed-specific healthy lifestyle, excellent care, balanced
nutrition, and adequate exercise.

An essential element of optimal preventive health care is regular observation and examination
of your dog. This requires that you familiarize yourself thoroughly with Kira's body and its
appearance in a healthy state so you can immediately detect any changes. A veterinary book on
canine health and one on canine first aid are indispensable. Equally important is a medicine cabinet
stocked according to your veterinarian's advice. A thorough health check (including urinalysis and
complete bloodwork) by the family veterinarian at least once a year, and more frequently as Kira
gets older, should be a matter of course.

Your veterinarian

Finding the right veterinarian for Kira is not an easy task; basically, however, the same
principles apply that you would use in choosing your own family physician. Of prime importance is
your confidence in the vet's professional competence—but never underrate the element of personal
rapport. Kira cannot be expected to enjoy going to the vet if she senses that you have an aversion to
that person. Interviewing other doggy people is certainly helpful, but the soundest decision is based
on personal impressions. It is best to visit the veterinarian at his or her practice and discuss openly
your intentions and concerns. A vet should always have sufficient time for every patient team
(Berner plus human). You should never have the feeling that you or your dog are being rushed.

Also, you must understand what the vet is doing with Kira and why. For a good vet, it is a matter of course to openly and fully inform his or her clients. One particularly significant question is whether the vet makes house calls. In that respect, distance also plays a role.

Once you have chosen your veterinarian and both you and Kira are happy with the person and his or her services, you should stay with that individual. For everyone involved (and, above all, for the dog), it is better than changing vets frequently. If you feel the need to get a second opinion in the case of a difficult diagnosis, a complicated condition, or an unsatisfactory healing process, you should openly discuss this with your family vet. By the same token, the vet should not hesitate to refer you to a colleague who is better qualified or equipped for certain conditions. The veterinary profession has recently undergone a distinct process of specialization. The diagnosis and treatment (especially surgery) of certain Berner-specific diseases may require such focused professional attention.

Regular visits to the vet build the puppy's trust and confidence

A visit to the veterinarian will normally not constitute any problem, since you gently familiarized Kira with the circumstances and gave her the opportunity to learn the appropriate behavior at puppy age. Unless it is an emergency, before leaving for the vet's Kira should be groomed (including her eyes, ears, and teeth) and taken for a short walk to relieve herself. If a urine sample is required, walk Kira on short leash and collect the urine in a suitable receptacle, such as a little pot with a handle or a ladle, as soon as she squats. In the waiting room, Kira should sit close to her human(s)—no sniffing at or playing with the other patients. Although some dogs will shiver fearfully or growl aggressively, a well-educated Bernese will live up to its reputation of being self-assured, dignified, and imperturbable. Because of their sterling character, Berners are usually very well-liked patients. To avoid the risk of injury, Kira is never allowed to jump onto the treatment table; instead, she is lifted up by you and the vet or the assistant. Throughout the examination, you should have hand or eye contact with Kira and talk to her in a calm, reassuring (but not pitying) tone. After the procedure, lift the dog down, praise her, and give her another treat. As a result of such consistently pleasant experiences, Kira will always return to the vet with a wagging tail.

Vaccinations

The vaccination protocol described here is current in German-speaking Europe. In other countries, different approaches (e.g., extension of intervals between boosters or titre tests) are being undertaken. Every Bernese puppy who comes from a recognized kennel is vaccinated at 8 weeks (before leaving the breeder's home) against distemper, hepatitis, leptospirosis, and parvovirus

(German: S for *Staupe,* H, L, P). This initial immunization will be complete and effective only if repeated four weeks later (at 12 weeks of age), and in the case of parvo eight weeks later (16 weeks). These booster vaccinations are the responsibility of the puppy buyer, as is the initial inoculation against rabies (German: *Tollwut*). In order to maintain the protective effect, some vaccinations must be repeated at one-year intervals (e.g., rabies) and others at two years. In Europe, rabies vaccinations must have been given not more than one year and not less than one month before traveling abroad or attending a dog show. Should Kira ever be left at a boarding kennel, she should be vaccinated against kennel cough (tracheobronchitis) at least four weeks prior to her stay (unless the annual combo-vacc already contains a vaccine against that disease). All vaccinations are recorded on an International Certificate of Vaccination which must accompany Kira to shows and on foreign travels.

Deworming

There is practically no puppy who is not afflicted with roundworms, hookworms, or whipworms. According to the regulations of the Berner breed clubs in German-speaking countries, puppies must be dewormed repeatedly before they leave their breeder. It is commonly recommended that the procedure be repeated at three-month intervals during the first year. After that—since deworming places considerable stress on the body—Kira should be treated only if there is a reasonable suspicion of infestation. As a precautionary measure, you should regularly submit stool samples to your veterinarian for examination. This is also important in the case of tapeworms, particularly the fox tapeworm, which has recently become widespread in central Europe and which is extremely dangerous to both dogs and their humans.

External parasites

External parasites (e.g., fleas, lice, mites, ticks) are not only unpleasant for the dog because of the skin irritation they cause (itching), but also because they constitute a serious health risk (viruses, infections, dermatoses). Infestation with parasites is not necessarily a result of poor hygiene; it may also be contracted through contact with other dogs (at playgrounds or shows) or different animals. In view of Kira's size and the thickness and length of her coat, the detection and treatment of skin parasites is a major problem. Insecticidal sprays and powders—which, because of their toxic nature, are risky anyway—are only of limited effectiveness. The same goes for flea or tick collars. Should Kira become heavily infested with parasites, a bath with an insecticidal shampoo may have to be considered.

An infestation of fleas (which are the intermediate hosts of tapeworms) can be detected by examining the dog's skin for little bumps, red spots, scabs, and tiny black specks (flea feces). Fleas invade not only the dog, but also its surroundings, especially its sleeping quarters. If the dog sleeps in several places around the house, considerable disinfection efforts become necessary.

While fleas are not abundant in German-speaking Europe, ticks are an especially serious problem. They can transmit a form of encephalitis that is equally dangerous for the dog and his humans. Ticks may also be carriers of *Lyme borreliosis,* a severe and complex disease that can affect the heart, eyes, joints, and nerves. Ticks tend to attack Kira's head (ear flaps, muzzle, eyebrows), throat, chest, armpits, and inner thighs. Within a few days, these tiny bloodsuckers grow to the size of a pea or small cherry and eventually drop off. A tick should never be pulled out, since the head is likely to remain in the skin, which may cause infection. Instead, they must be carefully twisted out with special tick tweezers that do not press against the body of the tick. In areas with a high risk of Lyme disease, administering a preventive medication (a vaccine is now also available) may have to be considered.

Specific health problems

A model patient

Practically every dog, regardless of breed, will suffer from a more or less serious health disorder at some time in his or her life. The Bernese Mountain Dog is no exception. Like any other dog, a Berner can get diarrhea, constipation, or a fever. A Berner, too, may vomit, contract an infection of the prepuce (balanoposthitis), develop an impaction of the anal sacs, or sprain a paw. Such things are a normal part of life and need not be discussed here. There are other, more severe diseases that may affect a Berner, just like any other dog. Such conditions— of the heart, lungs, skin, etc.—also do not require special mention here.

There are, however, health problems that seem to affect Berners more frequently than other breeds. As is true of other large-breed dogs, the normal life expectancy of a healthy Berner is 10 to 12 years. Several Bernese are known to have lived to 15 years of age; one German Berner even attained the age of 17 years. However, research conducted by Berner breed clubs in various countries on the dates and causes of Berner deaths yielded a statistical mean life expectancy of 7 to 8 years. Even though the overall picture may not be as gloomy as these figures suggest, anyone aiming to share their life with a Berner should be aware of and have at least a basic understanding of the health problems that exist in the breed. Some health problems that seem to be of concern to Berner people in other countries, such as PRA, vWD, and SAS are not seen in a sufficiently high incidence in German-speaking Europe to be considered a breed-specific problem; consequently, breeding stock is not screened for those conditions. However, it is a sad but undeniable fact that there are diseases that make many Berners suffer miserably, cause emotional hardship to their humans, and may constitute a heavy financial burden. Among these ailments are hip dysplasia, elbow dysplasia, cruciate ligament rupture, ectropion and entropion, torsion (bloat), and various types of cancer. What most of the above-mentioned diseases have in common is a fairly distinct genetic predisposition.

Hip dysplasia (HD)

The term "hip dysplasia" refers to an anomaly of the hip joint. In a healthy joint, the ball-shaped end of the thigh bone (femoral head) fits well into the concave hip socket (acetabulum). If, due to some growth irregularity, the articulating surfaces of the hip joint are misshapen (roughened, shallow, or flattened), they no longer match perfectly. Depending on the degree of abnormality, the hip joint will become increasingly unstable (subluxation); in extreme cases, the femoral head will slip out of the acetabulum. Due to the abnormal stress placed on the affected joint, hip dysplasia, which usually leads to arthrosis and arthritis, may cause considerable pain to the dog.

Contrary to popular belief, the disease cannot be diagnosed by external examination. The majority of affected dogs do not demonstrate any symptoms (such as lameness) mostly because good muscle tone compensates for the joint damage. A reliable diagnosis can only be made on the basis of radiography, and then only if the dog's skeletal system is fully developed. Hip dysplasia can neither be prevented nor cured. Depending upon the severity of the condition, treatment may range from the administration of analgesic and anti-inflammatory drugs to total hip replacement. Before subjecting a Berner to hip surgery, however, a second (and third) opinion should be sought. In an extreme case, euthanasia may even have to be considered.

Since hip dysplasia is an hereditary disease, Bernese breed clubs in German-speaking and other European countries have made radiography compulsory for all breeding stock. The minimum age ranges from 12 (SSV) to 14 (KBS) to 15 months (DCBS). For hip radiography in these countries, it is common practice (and required by the Berner clubs) that the dog be sedated or anesthesized to the point of total muscle relaxation (which must be certified by the x-raying vet), and two radiographs must be taken (one with the legs extended and one with legs flexed). In Germany, the radiographs must be submitted for evaluation to one veterinary radiologist designated by the breed club. In Switzerland, films are forwarded to the veterinary hospital at either the University of Bern or the University of Zürich. Evaluation of the films is based on recommendations issued by the FCI. The rating is recorded on the dog's pedigree and published in the respective club's Zuchtbuch. Hips are rated F, V, L, M, or S in Germany, which correspond to the FCI hip grades used in Switzerland: A (free of dysplasia), B (transitional), C (mild), D (moderate), and E (severe). In Switzerland, each hip is graded separately. Only dogs with one of the first three grades may be bred. A grade L (Switzerland: B, C) may only be bred to a grade F (Switzerland: A). Some European countries use split grades (A1, A2, B1, B2, etc.). According to the Orthopedic Foundation for Animals (OFA), the organization that evaluates canine joint status and maintains a registry in the United States, the FCI hip grades compare to OFA grades as follows: A1 = OFA Excellent; A2 = Good; B1 = Fair; B2 = Borderline; C = Mild; D = Moderate; E = Severe.

While compulsory radiography has undoubtedly lead to a decrease of hip dysplasia in Berners, the statistics must be taken with a grain of salt, given that only about twenty percent of the total dog population bred under the clubs' system is evaluated. Thus, there remains a high degree of uncertainty. It has to be assumed that, in at least some cases, x-rays of an obviously poor hip are not submitted for evaluation and thus do not appear in the breed statistics. Still, it would be foolish not to recognize the value of radiography. Every effort should be made to motivate as many people as possible to have their Berners x-rayed, even if the dogs do not show any clinical symptoms, and to submit the films for evaluation even if they demonstrate dysplasia. Breed clubs can only arrive at a valid assessment of the breed's state of health if a sufficient amount of data has been collected, and only then can they design and enforce appropriate steering mechanisms. In any case, Berner owners should only have their dog radiographed by a veterinarian who has experience in x-raying the hips of large dogs, then submit the films to their country's recognized organization for an authoritative assessment and rating, regardless of the experience and judgment of the veterinarian performing the radiography.

It is important to remember that breeding dogs with disease-free hips does not guarantee that all their offspring will be unaffected. Conversely, the consequences of non-genetic factors, such as malnutrition (excess protein, vitamins, and minerals) and/or excessive or inappropriate stress on the skeletal system (such as overweight, excessive exercise, jumping from heights, frequent climbing or descending of stairs, and roughhousing on slippery floors) are often overlooked, ignored, or underestimated. All of these factors may contribute to the development of joint disorders as well.

Elbow dysplasia (ED)

The term "elbow dysplasia" is commonly used to refer to a complex of diseases (osteochondroses) that affect the elbow joint. A differentiated description of the various degenerative manifestations cannot be provided here. Suffice it to say that the following abbreviations are also used: OCD (osteochondritis dissecans), UAP (ununited anconeal process), and FCP (fragmented coronoid process). In each case, the problem is a deformation of the bone or cartilage of the elbow joint resulting from growth irregularity, which produces excessive strain on particular parts of the joint. Frequently, minute cartilage and/or bone particles (called joint mouse) break off and float in the joint fluid, which causes the dog pain. Arthritis or arthrosis is usually the long-term result.

Elbow dysplasia originates from a predisposition to irregularities of skeletal growth, which affects Berners along with other large, fast-growing breeds. The development of the condition may—just as with HD—be triggered or exacerbated during the juvenile growth period by an imbalanced intake of protein, vitamins and minerals, and/or excessive stress placed on the bones and joints by excess weight or exercise.

Since research results suggest that there is a genetic predisposition also to elbow dysplasia, breed clubs in German speaking countries have made radiography mandatory for all breeding stock. The minimum age ranges from 12 (SSV) to 14 (KBS) to 15 months (DCBS). Only dogs with grade 0 or 1 will be admitted to the breed assessment.

Cruciate ligament rupture

The rupture of one or both cruciate ligaments in the knee is not uncommon in Bernese. The most obvious clinical symptom is a sudden limp, which may decrease in intensity but will usually not disappear completely. The rupture may occur after a sudden traumatic event such as a jump or a sudden twist. More often, however, a ligament that has been gradually damaged as a result of a degenerative, arthrotic deformation of the knee may partially or fully tear under even a minor strain (secondary rupture). It may be assumed that a connection exists between this disease and the breed-specific disposition to joint problems, as well as excess body weight. A ruptured cruciate ligament requires surgery, but full restoration of the knee's range of motion cannot be guaranteed.

Bloat

Like other large, deep-chested breeds, Berners are prone to bloat (acute gastric dilation or torsion). Males are affected more often than females. Bloat is a life-threatening condition that seems to occur most often (though not always) after the intake of a large quantity of food and/or water, which is followed by intense physical exercise. Stress may also be a factor.

In bloat, the stomach dilates due to the excessive formation of gas. This in itself can cause severe damage to arteries and veins in the abdomen, which can, in turn, result in circulatory shock. But the stomach may also twist upon itself, obstructing its entrance (esophagus) and exit (duodenum), thus trapping the excess gas. As a result of this torsion, the spleen may be displaced. Typical clinical signs of bloat are restlessness, salivation, excessive drooling, unsuccessful attempts to vomit, a distended abdomen, and, finally, circulatory shock. In almost all cases, emergency surgery is necessary to save the dog's life. A dog that has suffered one episode of bloat will be prone to recurrences.

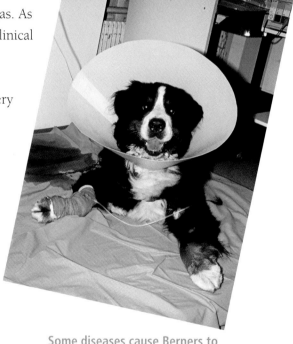

Entropion/ectropion

If a Berner has entropion, its eyelids will fit too tightly and will be more or less distinctly rolled inward. With every movement of the eyelid, the lashes rub the cornea, which causes painful irritation. Increased tear flow, chronic conjunctivitis, and chronic inflammation of the cornea with a subsequent risk of blindness are the long-term effects. Normally only surgical correction can solve the problem.

Some diseases cause Berners to suffer physically—and their humans to suffer emotionally

In ectropion, the eyelid is too loose. The lower lid will sag and roll outward, thus failing to protect the eyeball from air, dust, and germs. Again, chronic conjunctivitis will be the result, and corrective surgery may be required.

In cases of both entropion and ectropion, the decision for surgical correction should always be based on a second opinion, preferably that of a canine ophthalmologist. Such a step should not be taken until the Berner's skull is sufficiently developed. What may look like an ectropion on a puppy may well correct itself in the course of a few months. Since entropion and ectropion seem to be genetically determined, affected dogs must not be bred under the regulations of the Bernese breed clubs in German-speaking Europe.

Kidney failure

While kidney diseases are fairly common in all breeds, Berners seem to have an increased propensity for glomerulonephritis. This is a disease that damages the glomerula (the basic functional unit of the kidney), which in turn results in a loss of blood protein and eventually leads to chronic kidney failure. In many cases the disease is only discovered at an advanced stage, when it cannot be treated successfully.

Cancer

Research initiated by Berner breed clubs in Great Britain, the United States, Switzerland, and other countries has shown that an increasing number of Berners are dying at an alarmingly young age of various kinds of cancer. Although statistics should always be taken with a grain of salt and some of the evidence may be anecdotal, the findings must be taken seriously. The various forms of cancer that afflict Berners most often are malignant histiocytosis and lymphosarcoma. The former often begins as a swelling of the skin, metastasizes quickly, and often invades the visceral organs (liver, spleen, kidneys, lungs); the latter affects white blood cells (lymphocytes) which then produce tumors (primarily in the lymph nodes, bone marrow, and abdominal organs). While all other cancers are also found in other canine breeds, histiocytosis seems to occur exclusively in Berners. Even granted that environmental factors such as nutrition and pollution may play a part, research confirms that the breed displays a clear genetic disposition to this disease.

A Final Word

Bernese clubs in countries around the world have begun to fight genetic diseases. They have established health funds, support medical research projects, and maintain their own health databases. A successful war against hereditary forms of cancer and other genetic diseases cannot be fought without a sufficient quantity of good-quality data. It is therefore of utmost importance that as many Bernese people as possible—breeders and non-breeders alike—submit to their clubs information on all aspects of their beloved companions' health and death. In this context, the Berner-Garde database deserves special mention. This database was initiated by members of the San Francisco Bay Berners (SFBB), and the Berner-Garde Foundation was established in 1995. Dedicated Berner lovers generously and untiringly invest their expertise, energy, talent, time, and funds to maintain the Foundation and its work. The mission of Berner-Garde is to reduce the incidence of genetic disease. Access to information in the database is freely available worldwide via the Internet. Friends of Berners around the globe are urged to help the cause through participation in the collective efforts of their national Berner clubs and communities, as well as by their participation, use, and support of Berner-Garde. The Swiss Bernese Club (KBS) must be commended for organizing and hosting, in 2000 and 2002, the first international conferences on Berner health. Delegates from Berner clubs around the world participated in the events. Hopefully, these events will become a regular part of Bernerdom worldwide.

The privilege of living with a Bernese Mountain Dog is a priceless gift. Life with a Berner Sennenhund, whether it lasts 1, 5, 7, or 12 years, is a blessing and a dream. Every Berner person can and must do their share to make the dream last as long as possible by providing their Bäri with a healthy environment, nourishing food, a wholesome lifestyle, optimal preventive healthcare, and lots of TLC. Still, for many, the dream may be all too short-lived. It is the obligation of each and every breeder to be aware of the existing health problems and to fight them through his or her own breeding program. Breed clubs are obligated to recognize and combat these health problems through a collective global effort that includes relevant education and, where necessary and possible, appropriate steering policies and mechanisms. It the obligation of all those who enjoy the blessing of sharing their lives with a Berner to support their breeders' and their clubs' efforts in every way they can. All of them—all of us—are responsible for doing everything in our respective powers to ensure that every one of these glorious creatures enjoys a long, healthy, and happy life, providing their humans with the joy and happiness that only the most wonderful canine companion in the world can give: the Bernese Mountain Dog—the dog of destiny.

Beauty

Winter is truly the Berner's favorite season. When the temperature falls, a Berner's spirit rises. Anyone who has ever watched a Berner romping on a crisp day, rolling in a frost-covered meadow, catching snowflakes in the air, leaping and diving through powdery drifts, or turning somersaults and skidding on his back knows that winter is Berner heaven. Take your Berner buddy out on a cold, sunny, snowy, stormy, foggy, or frosty winter day and let yourself be overwhelmed by the breathtaking, awe-inspiring beauty of the Bernese Mountain Dog.

The joy of life

The AKC Standard for the Bernese Mountain Dog

General Appearance

The Bernese Mountain Dog is a striking, tri-colored, large dog. He is sturdy and balanced. He is intelligent, strong and agile enough to do the draft and droving work for which he was used in the mountainous regions of his origin. Dogs appear masculine, while bitches are distinctly feminine.

Size, Proportion, Substance

Measured at the withers, dogs are 25 to 27½ inches; bitches are 23 to 26 inches. Though appearing square, Bernese Mountain Dogs are slightly longer in body than they are tall. Sturdy bone is of great importance. The body is full.

Head

Expression is intelligent, animated and gentle. The eyes are dark brown and slightly oval in shape with close-fitting eyelids. Inverted or everted eyelids are serious faults. Blue eye color is a disqualification. The ears are medium sized, set high, triangular in shape, gently rounded at the tip, and hang close to the head when in repose. When the Bernese Mountain Dog is alert, the ears are brought forward and raised at the base; the top of the ear is level with the top of the skull. The skull is flat on top and broad, with a slight furrow and a well-defined, but not exaggerated, stop. The muzzle is strong and straight. The nose is always black. The lips are clean and, as the Bernese Mountain Dog is a dry-mouthed breed, the flews are only slightly developed. The teeth meet in a scissors bite. An overshot or undershot bite is a serious fault. Dentition is complete.

Neck, Topline, Body

The neck is strong, muscular and of medium length. The topline is level from the withers to the croup. The chest is deep and capacious with well-sprung, but not barrel shaped, ribs and brisket reaching at least to the elbows. The back is broad and firm. The loin is strong. The croup is broad and smoothly rounded to the tail insertion. The tail is bushy. It should be carried low when in repose. An upward swirl is permissible when the dog is alert, but the tail may never curl or be carried over the back. The bones in the tail should feel straight and should reach to the hock joint or below. A kink in the tail is a fault.

Forequarters

The shoulders are moderately laid back, flat-lying, well-muscled and never loose. The legs are straight and strong and the elbows are well under the shoulder when the dog is standing. The pasterns slope very slightly, but are never weak. Dewclaws may be removed. The feet are round and compact with well-arched toes.

Hindquarters

The thighs are broad, strong and muscular. The stifles are moderately bent and taper smoothly into the hocks. The hocks are well let down and straight as viewed from the rear. Dewclaws should be removed. Feet are compact and turn neither in nor out.

Coat

The coat is thick, moderately long and slightly wavy or straight. It has a bright natural sheen. Extremely curly or extremely dull-looking coats are undesirable. The Bernese Mountain Dog is shown in natural coat and undue trimming is to be discouraged.

Color and Markings

The Bernese Mountain Dog is tri-colored. The ground color is jet black. The markings are rich rust and clear white. Symmetry of markings is desired. Rust appears over each eye, on the cheeks reaching to at least the corner of the mouth, on each side of the chest, on all four legs, and under the tail. There is a white blaze and muzzle band. A white marking on the chest typically forms an inverted cross. The tip of the tail is white. White on the feet is desired but must not extend higher than the pasterns. Markings other than described are to be faulted in direct relationship to the extent of the deviation. White legs or a white collar are serious faults. Any ground color other than black is a disqualification.

Gait

The natural working gait of the Bernese Mountain Dog is a slow trot. However, in keeping with his use in draft and droving work, he is capable of speed and agility. There is good reach in front. Powerful drive from the rear is transmitted through a level back. There is no wasted action. Front and rear legs on each side follow through in the same plane. At increased speed, legs tend to converge toward the center line.

Temperament

The temperament is self-confident, alert and good natured, never sharp or shy. The Bernese Mountain Dog should stand steady, though may remain aloof to the attentions of strangers.

Disqualifications

Blue eye color.

Any ground color other than black.

(Approved February 10, 1990. Effective March 28, 1990. Reproduced with the kind permission of the Bernese Mountain Dog Club of America.)

■ The CKC Standard for the Bernese Mountain Dog

General Appearance

Large, sturdy, well-balanced working dog of substantial bone. Square in appearance from withers to ground and withers to tail set. Heavy-coated with distinctive characteristic markings. In comparison with the opposite sex, dogs appear masculine, bitches feminine without loss of type.

Temperament

The Bernese temperament is one of the breed's strongest assets. Consistent, dependable, with a strong desire to please. Self-confident, alert, good natured. Attached and loyal to human family; may be aloof or suspicious with strangers, but never sharp or shy. A dog must stand for examination when required to do so by his handler.

Size

Dogs 24.4–27.6 inches (62–70 cm), best size 26–26.8 inches (66–68 cm); bitches 22.8–26 inches (58–66 cm), best size 23.6–24.8 inches (60–63 cm). Height measured at withers. The stocky, well-balanced appearance must be maintained.

Coat and colour

The adult coat is thick, moderately long, possibly with a slight wave but never curly. It has a bright natural sheen. In texture it is soft rather than harsh, but is weather resistant, easily kept and resists matting. There is a soft, seasonal undercoat. Compulsory markings: Jet-black ground colour. Rich russet markings (dark reddish brown is most favoured) appear on the cheeks, in a spot over each eye, in a patch above each foreleg, and on all four legs between the black of the upper leg and the white of the feet. Clean white markings as follows: On chest extending uninterrupted to under chin; also a slight- to middle-sized blaze extending into a muzzle band which is not so wide as to obliterate the russet on the cheek (and which preferably does not extend past the corners of the mouth). Preferable markings: White feet with white reaching at the highest the pasterns and a white tip of tail. Marking should be symmetrical. Too little white is preferable to too much.

Head

Skull—Flat and broad with a slight furrow; defined, but not exaggerated stop. Muzzle—strong and straight; roughly square proportions, tapering only very slightly. Muzzle is slightly shorter than length of skull. Lips are fairly clean and tight; black in colour. Teeth—jaw is strong with good teeth meeting in a scissors bite. Dentition should be complete. Nostrils—well open and black in colour. Eyes—dark brown in colour, almond shaped, and well set apart; tight eyelids. Expression is intelligent, animated and gentle. Ears—middle-sized triangular in shape with rounded tip. Set above eye level high on side of head; hanging close to the head in repose, brought forward at the base when alert.

Neck

Strong, muscular, of medium length, well set on. Dew-laps are very slightly developed.

Forequarters

Shoulders are well muscled, flat lying and well laid back. Forelegs are straight with substantial bone; parallel stance. Elbows are well under shoulders. Pasterns are slightly sloping, but not weak. Feet are proportionate in size, round and compact. Dewclaws are preferably removed.

Body

Approximately square from withers to ground and withers to tail set. The body is sturdy. The chest is broad, with good depth of brisket reaching at least to the elbows; ribs are well sprung. The back is firm and level. Loins are strong and muscular. The croup is broad, well muscled.

Hindquarters

The hindquarters are powerful, with broad, well-muscled thighs and substantial bone. Stifles are well angulated. Hocks are well let down, turning neither in nor out. Pasterns are wide and straight, standing parallel. Feet are proportionate in size, round and compact. Dewclaws must be removed in the first few days of life.

Tail

Bushy, hanging straight, with bone reaching to the hock joint or slightly below. Carried low in repose, higher when the dog is in motion or alert. An upward arc is permissible, but the tail should never curl over itself or be carried over the back.

Gait

The natural traveling gait of the breed is a slow trot, but it is capable of speed and agility. Good reach in front. Strong drive from the rear, flexing well at the stifles. The level backline is maintained; there is no wasted action. Front and rear feet of each side travel in lines parallel to direction of motion, converging towards a centre line at increased speeds.

Faults

A fault is any deviation from the standard, to be weighed in accordance with the degree of deviation. In addition and in particular: Major faults: ectropion or entropion; undershot or overshot mouth; tail rolled over back. Minor faults (subject to degree of fault): deficiency of type, particularly lack of substance; overly long or thin body; light or round eyes; level bite; incomplete dentition; too narrow or too snipey muzzle; too massive or too light head; too light russet markings or impure colour; grey colouring in black coat; nonsymmetrical markings, especially facial; white neck patch; white anal patch; curly coat in adult dog; splayed feet; kink in tail.

Disqualifications

Cryptorchid or monorchid males; split nose; absent markings as described in compulsory markings; white neck ring; blue eye; ground colour other than black.

(This Breed Standard has been reproduced with the kind permission of The Canadian Kennel Club. www.ckc.ca)

■ The KC Standard for the Bernese Mountain Dog

General Appearance

Strong, sturdy working dog, active, alert, well boned, of striking colour.

Characteristics

A multi-purpose farm dog capable of draught work. A kind and devoted family dog. Slow to mature.

Temperament

Self-confident, good-natured, friendly and fearless. Aggressiveness not to be tolerated.

Head and Skull

Strong with flat skull, very slight furrow, well defined stop; strong straight muzzle. Lips slightly developed.

Eyes

Dark brown, almond-shaped, well fitting eyelids.

Ears

Medium-sized; set high, triangular-shaped, lying flat in repose, when alert brought slightly forward and raised at base.

Mouth

Jaws strong with a perfect, regular and complete scissor bite, i.e. upper teeth closely overlapping lower teeth and set square to the jaws.

Neck

Strong, muscular and medium length.

Forequarters

Shoulders long, strong and sloping, with upper arm forming a distinct angle, flat lying, well muscled. Forelegs straight from all sides. Pasterns flexing slightly.

Body

Compact rather than long. Height to length 9:10. Broad chest, good depth of brisket reaching at least to elbow. Well ribbed; strong loins. Firm, straight back. Rump smoothly rounded.

Hindquarters

Broad, strong and well muscled. Stifles well bent. Hock strong, well let down and turning neither in nor out. Dewclaws to be removed.

Feet

Short, round and compact.

Tail

Bushy, reaching just below hock. Raised when alert or moving but never curled or carried over back.

Gait/Movement

Stride reaching out well in front, following well through behind, balanced stride in all gaits.

Coat

Soft, silky with bright natural sheen, long, slightly wavy but should not curl when mature.

Colour

Jet black, with rich reddish-brown on cheeks, over eyes, on all four legs and on chest. Slight to medium-sized symmetrical white head marking (blaze) and white chest marking (cross) are essential. Preferred but not essential: white paws, white not reaching higher than pastern, white tip to tail. A few white hairs at nape of neck, and white anal patch undesirable but tolerated.

Size

Height: dogs: 64–70 cm (25–27½ in.); bitches: 58–66 cm (23–26 in.).

Faults

Any departure from the foregoing points should be considered a fault and the seriousness with which the fault should be regarded should be in exact proportion to its degree and its effect upon the health and welfare of the dog.

Note

Male animals should have two apparently normal testicles fully descended into the scrotum.

(March 1994. Copyright the Kennel Club. Reproduced with their kind permission.)

■ The NZKC Standard for the Bernese Mountain Dog

Characteristics:

Self confident, good natured. Aggressiveness must not be tolerated. Slow to mature.

General Appearance:

Above medium sized, strong, sturdy working dog, active, alert, well boned, of striking colour.

Head and Skull:

Strong with flat skull and slightly developed furrow, well defined stop, strong straight muzzle. Lips slightly developed.

Eyes:

Dark brown and almond-shaped, eyelids tight.

Ears:

Medium sized ears, set high, triangular shaped, lying flat in repose, when alert brought slightly forward, and raised at the base.

Mouth:

Scissor bite.

Neck:

Strong, muscular and of medium length.

Forequarters:

Shoulders long, strong and sloping, with the upper arm forming a distinct angle, flat lying and well muscled. Appears straight from all sides.

Body:

Compact rather than long. Ratio height to length 9:10. Broad chest, with good depth of brisket, reaching at least to the elbow. Well-ribbed; strong loins. Back firm and straight. Rump smoothly rounded.

Hindquarters:

Quarters broad, strong and well-muscled. Stifles well bent. Hock strong, well let down and turning neither in nor out. Dewclaws should be removed.

Feet:

Short, round and compact.

Gait:

Stride reaching out well in front, following well through behind, balanced stride in all gaits.

Tail:

Bushy, reaching just below the hock; may be raised when dog alert or moving but never curled or carried above the level of the back.

Temperament:

Self confident, good natured, friendly and fearless.

Coat:

Soft and silky with bright natural sheen, long and slightly wavy, but should not be curly when mature.

Colour:

Jet black, with rich reddish brown on the cheeks, over the eyes, on all four legs and on chest. Slight to medium sized symmetrical white head marking (blaze) and white chest marking (cross) are essential. Preferred but not essential: white paws, white not reaching higher than the pastern, white tip to tail. A few white hairs at nape of neck and white anal patch undesirable but tolerated.

Height and Size:

Dogs: 64–70 cm (25–27.5 in.) at the withers, preferred size 66–68 cm (26–26.7 in.) Bitches: 58–66 cm (23–26 in.) at the withers, preferred size 60–63 cm (23.5–25 in.).

Faults:

Any departure from the foregoing points should be considered a fault and the seriousness of the fault should be in exact proportion to its degree.

Note:

Male animals should have two apparently normal testicles fully descended into the scrotum.

(Reproduced with the kind permission of the New Zealand Kennel Club.)

Useful Addresses

■ **National Bernese Mountain Dog Clubs in German- and English-speaking countries**

Note: The addresses of further national and many regional BMD clubs/communities can be obtained from the Web sites listed below and/or from the Kennel Club of the respective country.

Austria

Verein für Schweizer Sennenhunde in Österreich (VSSÖ)
www.sennenhunde.org/at

Canada

Bernese Mountain Dog Club of Canada (BMDCC)
www.bmdcc.ca

Germany

Deutscher Club für Berner Sennenhunde e.V. (DCBS)
www.dcbs.de
Schweizer Sennenhund-Verein für Deutschland e.V. (SSV)
www.ssv-ev.de

Great Britain

Bernese Mountain Dog Club of Great Britain (BMDCGB)
www.bernese.co.uk

Switzerland

Schweizerischer Klub für Berner Sennenhunde (KBS)
www.bernersennenhund.ch

United States of America

Bernese Mountain Dog Club of America
www.bmdca.org

■ **National Kennel Clubs in German- and English-speaking countries**

International Federation of Kennel Clubs

Fédération Cynologique Internationale (FCI)
www.fci.be

Austria

Österreichischer Kynologenverband (ÖKV)
www.oekv.at

Australia

Australian National Kennel Council (ANKC)
www.ankc.aust.com

Canada

Canadian Kennel Club (CKC)

www.ckc.ca

Germany

Verband für das Deutsche Hundewesen (VDH)

www.vdh.de

Great Britain

The Kennel Club (KC)

www.the-kennel-club.org.uk

Ireland (IKC)

The Irish Kennel Club

www.ikc.ie

New Zealand

New Zealand Kennel Club (NZKC)

www.nzkc.org.nz

South Africa

The Kennel Union of Southern Africa (KUSA)

www.kusa.co.za

Switzerland

Schweizerische Kynologische Gesellschaft (SKG)

www.hundeweb.org

United States of America

American Kennel Club (AKC)

www.akc.org

■ Selected Web Sites

The Bernese Mountain Dog Home Page
www.berner.org

Berner Garde
www.bernergarde.org

The Internet Bernese Mountain Dog Consortium's PandaSite
http://bernesebreeders.org

Zuchtverband für Schweizer Hunderassen (Federation of Swiss Breeds)
www.zvsh.ch

The Natural History Museum, Bern
www.nmbe.ch/deutsch/531_5_3.html

■ Selected E-mail Groups

Note: A more comprehensive list of e-mail groups can be found at *http://groups.yahoo.com*

http://groups.yahoo.com/group/Berner-l/
http://groups.yahoo.com/group/bernese-in-gb/
http://groups.yahoo.com/group/berneseinoz/
http://groups.yahoo.com/group/NaturalBerners/

Bibliography—Selected Reading

Bärtschi, Margret, and Hansjoachim Spengler. *Hunde sehen - züchten - erleben: das Buch vom Berner Sennenhund.* Bern; Stuttgart: Haupt, 1992.

Cochrane, Diana. *The Bernese Mountain Dog.* Rev. ed. Haselor Hill, 1987.

Crawford, Julia M. *The Bernese Mountain Dog.* Foster City, CA: Howell, 2000.

Guenter, Bernd. *Berner Sennenhund.* 5th ed. Mürlenbach: Kynos, 2004.

Heim, Albert. *Die Schweizer Sennenhunde.* Zürich: Albert Müller, 1914.

Räber, Hans. *Die Schweizer Hunderassen.* 2nd ed. Rüschlikon: Albert Müller, 1980.

Russ, Diane, and Shirley Rogers. *The Beautiful Bernese Mountain Dog.* Loveland, CO: Alpine, 1993.

Simonds, Jude. *The Complete Bernese Mountain Dog.* Letchworth: Ringpress, 1989.

Smith, Sharon Chesnutt. *The New Bernese Mountain Dog.* New York: Howell, 1995.

Willis, Malcolm B. *The Bernese Mountain Dog Today.* Lydney: Ringpress Book, 1998.

The Bernese Mountain Dog Annual. Wheat Ridge, CO: Hoflin, 1994 ff.

■ Selected club publications:

Deutscher Club für Berner Sennenhunde, *Zuchtbuch*

Schweizer Sennenhund-Verein für Deutschland, *Zucht-, Kör- und Leistungsbuch*

Schweizerischer Klub für Berner Sennenhunde, *Zucht- und Körbuch*

Verein für Schweizer Sennenhunde in Österreich, *Zuchtbuch*

Bernese Mountain Dog Club of America, *The Bernese Mountain Dog Handbook.* 1994

Bernese Mountain Dog Club of America, *The Illustrated Standard of the Bernese Mountain Dog.* 2nd ed., 2001

Bernese Mountain Dog Club of America, *Yearbook*

Bernese Mountain Dog Club of America, *The Alpenhorn*

Bernese Mountain Dog Club of Canada, *Bernese Please*

Bernese Mountain Dog Club of Great Britain, *Magazine*

Bernese Mountain Dog Club of Great Britain, *Handbook*

■ List of Abbreviations

AKC   American Kennel Club

ANKC   Australian National Kennel Council

BMDCA   Bernese Mountain Dog Club of America

BMDCC   Bernese Mountain Dog Club of Canada

BMDCGB   Bernese Mountain Dog Club of Great Britain

CAC   *Certificat d'Aptitude au Championat*

CACIB   *Certificat d'Aptitude au Championat International de Beauté*

CKC   Canadian Kennel Club

DCBS   *Deutscher Club für Berner Sennenhunde* (one of two German Breed Clubs;
            the other is the SSV)

FCI   *Fédération Cynologique Internationale*

IKC   Irish Kennel Club

KBS   *Schweizerischer Klub für Berner Sennenhunde* (Swiss Breed Club)

KC   Kennel Club

KUSA   Kennel Union of South Africa

NZKC   New Zealand Kennel Club

ÖKV   *Österreichischer Kynologenverband* (Austrian Kennel Club)

SHSB   *Schweizerisches Hundestammbuch* (Swiss Kennel Club registry)

SKG   *Schweizerische Kynologische Gesellschaft* (Swiss Kennel Club)

SSV   *Schweizer Sennenhund-Verein für Deutschland* (one of two German Breed Clubs;
            the other is the DCBS)

VDH   *Verband für das Deutsche Hundewesen* (German Kennel Club)

VSSÖ   *Verein für Schweizer Sennenhunde in Österreich* (Austrian Breed Club)